Caribou Monitoring Protocol for the Arctic Network Inventory and Monitoring Program

Natural Resource Technical Report NPS/ARCN/NRR—2012/564

Kyle Joly

National Park Service
Gates of the Arctic National Park and Preserve
Arctic Network Inventory and Monitoring Program
4175 Geist Road
Fairbanks, AK 99709

Scott D. Miller

National Park Service
Arctic Network Inventory and Monitoring Program
4175 Geist Road
Fairbanks, AK 99709

Brad S. Shults

National Park Service
Western Arctic Parklands
4175 Geist Road
Fairbanks, AK 99709

August 2012

U.S. Department of the Interior
National Park Service
Natural Resource Stewardship and Science
Fort Collins, Colorado

The National Park Service, Natural Resource Stewardship and Science office in Fort Collins, Colorado publishes a range of reports that address natural resource topics of interest and applicability to a broad audience in the National Park Service and others in natural resource management, including scientists, conservation and environmental constituencies, and the public.

The Natural Resource Report Series is used to disseminate high-priority, current natural resource management information with managerial application. The series targets a general, diverse audience, and may contain NPS policy considerations or address sensitive issues of management applicability.

All manuscripts in the series receive the appropriate level of peer review to ensure that the information is scientifically credible, technically accurate, appropriately written for the intended audience, and designed and published in a professional manner.

This report received formal peer review by subject-matter experts who were not directly involved in the collection, analysis, or reporting of the data, and whose background and expertise put them on par technically and scientifically with the authors of the information.

Views, statements, findings, conclusions, recommendations, and data in this report do not necessarily reflect views and policies of the National Park Service, U.S. Department of the Interior. Mention of trade names or commercial products does not constitute endorsement or recommendation for use by the U.S. Government.

This report is available from the Arctic Network Inventory and Monitoring Program (http://science.nature.nps.gov/im/units/arcn) and the Natural Resource Publications Management website (http://www.nature.nps.gov/publications/nrpm).

Please cite this publication as:

Joly, K., S. D. Miller and B. S. Shults. 2012. Caribou monitoring protocol for the Arctic Network Inventory and Monitoring Program. Natural Resource Report NPS/ARCN/NRR—2012/564. National Park Service, Fort Collins, Colorado.

NPS 953/116691, August 2012

Contents

Contents (continued)

Contents (continued)

Contents (continued)

Contents (continued)

Contents (continued)

Executive Summary

Caribou (*Rangifer tarandus*) are an integral part of the ecological and cultural fabric of northwest Alaska. The Western Arctic Herd (WAH) caribou roam over this entire region, including all 5 Arctic Network Inventory and Monitoring Program (ARCN) National Park Units. Conservation of healthy caribou populations are specifically mentioned within the enabling legislation (Alaska National Interested Lands Conservation Act or ANILCA) of three of these Parks and is of critical concern of subsistence hunters within this region. Caribou are, by far, the most abundant large mammal in northwest Alaska and are famous for their long-distance migrations and large population oscillations. For these reasons, ARCN chose WAH caribou as a Vital Sign.

This report documents the protocols ARCN will utilize to help monitor this herd. Principal among them is the use of Geographic Positioning System (GPS) radiotelemetry collars that are capable of transmitting location data to a satellite. Given the extremely remote area which the WAH inhabits, this system provides the most efficient and accurate means to track individual caribou. These data will be utilized to monitor the timing and location of migrations, as well as seasonal distributions of WAH caribou. Monitoring phenology is perhaps the simplest means to track the influence of climate change, natural perturbations, development, and other potential impacts on a species.

These protocols also document the National Park Service's commitment and involvement with the WAH Working Group. The group is comprised of important stakeholders, including representatives for rural villages, sport hunters, conservationists, guides, transporters, and reindeer herders. All of the agencies charged with managing the WAH, including the National Park Service, US Fish and Wildlife Service, Bureau of Land Management and Alaska Department of Fish and Game, serve as advisors to the group. Information gathered by the Caribou Vital Sign are intended to supplement and complement existing data streams gather by the other cooperating agencies and should be of vital importance in future management decisions.

Acknowledgments

Assistance, contributions and/or previous research by Perry Barboza (UAF), Kimberlee Beckman (ADFG), Jim Dau (ADFG), Steve Fancy (NPS), Dave Gustine (USGS), and Sandra Talbot (USGS), as well as reviews by Brad Griffith (USGS), Anne Orlando (FWS) and Grant Hilderbrand (NPS) greatly improved previous drafts of the protocols for this Vital Sign.

Introduction and Objectives

Issue being Addressed and Rationale for Monitoring Caribou

This narrative is designed to introduce a caribou monitoring protocol for the Arctic Network (ARCN), which contains five units of the U. S. National Park system: Gates of the Arctic Park and Preserve (GAAR); Noatak National Preserve (NOAT); Cape Krusenstern National Monument (CAKR), Kobuk Valley National Park (KOVA) and Bering Land Bridge National Preserve (BELA). This narrative is accompanied by core standard operating procedures (SOPs) that describe in detail the techniques to be used in monitoring caribou.

Caribou (*Rangifer tarandus*), occur in all five network parks and are a keystone large mammal species in Arctic Alaska. Of the various Arctic caribou herds, only the Western Arctic Herd (WAH) regularly utilizes all 5 park units. Caribou are of great importance to people from both consumptive and non-consumptive viewpoints, and to the ecosystem as a whole. At an estimated population size of over 490,000 animals in 2003 (Dau 2007), the WAH is a significant ecological force in northwest Alaska and is the largest caribou herd in the state. The most recent estimates (325,000 caribou in 2011; J. Dau, *personal communication*) have shown the herd to be in decline from the 2003 population peak. The WAH has a substantial cultural impact in that the heritage and traditions of Native Alaskans in approximately 40 subsistence based communities in the region have been shaped by the availability of these caribou (Western Arctic Herd Working Group 2003). The availability of WAH also affects the economics of this region. The presence and relative abundance of WAH caribou have substantial impacts on the populations of wolves, bears, and wolverines in the area. Caribou are good integrators of regional conditions in northwestern Alaska because of their migratory nature. Caribou may have substantial effects on plant and lichen communities and by extension wildlife communities, either directly through browsing and grazing or indirectly through biogeochemical cycling. Key reasons for monitoring the WAH in network parks are that caribou; (1) are an extremely important subsistence species that occur in all park units within this network; (2) are specifically identified in the enabling legislation of GAAR, KOVA and NOAT; (3) directly impact reindeer and reindeer herders in BELA; (4) are considered good indicators of the condition of park ecosystems because they consume lichens and fungi making them good bio-indicators of environmental toxins; and (5) national and international datasets exist for comparison of caribou herds and caribou ecology across the Arctic region.

Caribou are a species specifically identified in the enabling legislation and management objectives of three of five the Arctic Network parks (U. S. Congress 1980). This legislation states that the National Park Service (NPS) will manage this species for natural and healthy populations. Caribou are of great importance to park visitors because of the opportunities to view caribou in Alaskan parks. The WAH also represents an ever rarer natural phenomenon in this country and indeed the world, the functioning migration of a large land mammal. While the primary objectives of monitoring will be to track the distribution of caribou, a variety of accessory data will be obtained in the monitoring process, that are likely to have great value for wildlife management, research and evaluating long-term changes in the WAH.

Historical Development of Caribou Monitoring

Scientific studies of Alaska caribou began with ground-based observational studies, including the landmark research of Olaus Murie (1935) and Ronald Skoog (1968). Aerial photographic censuses of the WAH began in 1970 (Davis et al. 1980) and have continued until the present (Dau 2007). Conventional radio telemetry equipment greatly increased the ability of biologists to track and enumerate caribou and is still in wide use. Satellite telemetry has allowed biologist to follow the movements of caribou during inclement weather and the short days of winter. Relatively recently, the fusion of Geographic Positioning System (GPS) and satellite technology has allowed for remote monitoring of caribou with greater spatial accuracy. GPS-satellite telemetry had not been utilized on the WAH prior to the development of this protocol.

The Alaska Department of Fish and Game (ADFG) is the lead agency in the monitoring of the WAH and currently it collects the following data on the WAH: population size (photo-censuses), blood (disease screening, genetics), calf weights in fall, fall composition counts, recruitment (short yearling) surveys, neonate counts, movement and distribution, survivorship, and health assessments. Blood and calf weight are obtained at Onion Portage (Kobuk National Park) during an annual capture operation. Department of Interior agencies (NPS, US Fish and Wildlife Service [FWS], and Bureau of Land Management [BLM]) have contributed to ADFG's efforts to monitor and manage the herd. The intent of this monitoring protocol is to complement and enhance the existing monitoring efforts lead by the ADFG. Fully collaborative and cooperative interagency partnerships have been recommended as a blueprint for effective monitoring and management by Circum-Arctic Rangifer Monitoring and Assessment Network (CARMA) and the North Slope Science Initiative (NSSI).

Measurable Objectives – Core Program

- Capture and radio collar WAH caribou to maintain a sample size of 30-40 GPS collars.
- Obtain frequent (>2/day) location data via GPS-satellite telemetry.
- Membership, attendance and activity on the WAH Working Group Technical Committee.
- Attendance and involvement at WAH Working Group meetings.
- Obtain herd and environmental conditions data by radio tracking in October and April.
- Define seasonal ranges (calving, insect relief, summer, winter).
- Define migratory corridors.
- Detect changes in range distribution over time.
- Detect changes in survivorship over time.
- Detect changes in migration routes and phenology over time.
- Detect changes in the location and timing of calving (using GPS data).

Sampling Design

Rationale for Selecting this Sampling Design Over Others

Caribou are a difficult species to monitor. They are highly vagile and exhibit extreme variability in their occurrence, distribution, density and numbers. The WAH inhabits the most remote park lands in the country. Radio telemetry, especially satellite-based systems, allow biologist to track the movements and assist in the enumeration of herds. Satellite telemetry systems have many advantages over conventional telemetry systems that require aircraft to locate individuals. Aerial radio tracking flights are limited by weather and daylight, where satellite systems are not limited by these factors. On a per location basis, satellite systems are cost effective, especially in extremely remote areas such as northwest Alaska. Telemetry monitoring systems do have drawbacks. They do not convey information about the health of the animal, status of off-spring, nor the number of caribou that are with the collared individual. Handling individual caribou allows for the collection of data about body condition, disease prevalence, contaminant loads, and genetics. A combination of satellite telemetry, aerial surveys and hands-on measurements provides a diversity of information streams that is well suited for the complexities of managing caribou in northwest Alaska. The immense range and seasonally variable concentrations of caribou, in combination with the extremely remote environment in which they thrive, are not conducive to non-invasive methods of monitoring such as track surveys and hair snares (genetic studies).

Site Selection

Site selection will be determined by the movements of the WAH. The herd ranges over 360,000 square kilometers of northwest Alaska (Dau 2007). The distribution of the herd changes annually and thus a study area with definitive, set boundaries is not appropriate. The herd calves in the Utukok uplands and migrates south across the Kobuk River consistently. The herd has exploited new winter ranges concurrent with its numerical expansion from 1976-2003. The WAH, while vitally important to the ecosystems of the parks in the Arctic Network and its users, spends much of its time outside the boundaries of these units. Monitoring must take place at the level of the herd in order to get a reasonable picture of population-level processes.

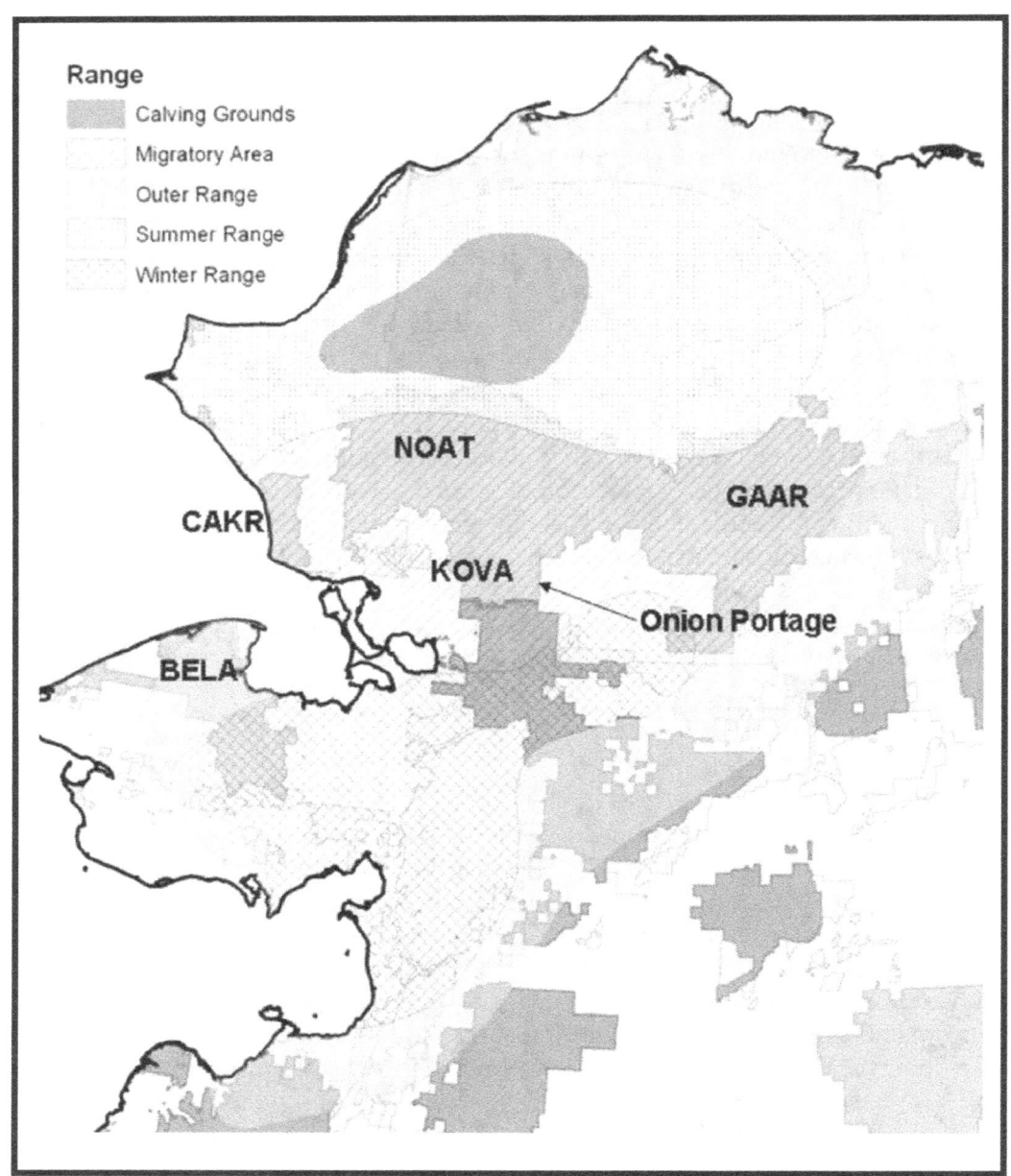

Figure 1. Range of the population (e.g., the Western Arctic Caribou Herd) being monitored.

Population Being Monitored

Three caribou herds (WAH, Teshekpuk Caribou Herd [TCH], and Central Arctic Herd [CAH]) utilize park lands within the Arctic Network. As opportunity and needs arise, cooperative efforts will be pursued to learn more about all of these herds. Only the WAH, however, utilizes all 5 park units consistently on a regular basis. The WAH, as of 2011, was also the largest of these herds; with more caribou than all of the other arctic Alaska (TCH, CAH, and Porcupine Caribou Herd) herds combined. Approximately 15,000 caribou are harvested annually by rural subsistence hunters from 40 villages in northwest Alaska (Dau 2007). For these reasons, monitoring the WAH is the most logical choice for the Arctic Network. There is also a need for data on the other arctic herds, but these herds have experienced greater levels of development pressure and thus have teams of biologists working to collect data on them. It would not be practical for the Arctic Network to collect enough data on all these herds to be useful, thus, this protocol attempts to strike a balance by collecting enough data for determining trends but limits that data collection to a single herd (i.e., the WAH). Because habitat, predator populations, weather conditions and management regimes vary widely across Alaska, no monitoring effort will be representative of caribou populations across the state, or across the Arctic Network.

Numerous data streams are being and have been collected by the ADFG for decades (Dau 2007). These data have provided users and managers of the herd an important overview of the demograhy of the herd. Full implementation of the monitoring protocol will enhance existing data streams and fill in missing pieces of the existing monitoring effort.

Sampling Frequency and Replication

Collared caribou will be located at least twice per day using satellite GPS technology. GPS collars will initially be programmed to take 3 locations per day with data uploaded through the ARGOS satellite system during protocol development. The use of GPS collars will greatly facilitate the determination of seasonal ranges, migration routes, timing of migration and survivorship, so that aerial tracking flights may be reduced to a minimum. Mortality of collared caribou requires that collars must be replaced on an ongoing basis so additional collars will be deployed annually to maintain sample size. Capture of caribou for radio collaring will likely be conducted in September at Onion Portage. Additional monitoring, in the form of aerial survey flights will be conducted, generally in October and April.

Detectable Level of Change

The size of the WAH has been found to fluctuate from 75,000 to nearly half a million caribou (Dau 2007). Thus, it is challenging to identify truly unusual changes in population levels. The mortality data from collared caribou, along with herd composition, body condition, genetic, disease, and behavioral information can provide clues to the causes of population changes and all may be useful in evaluating management actions. The detailed and high frequency location data will be utilized to determined changes in seasonal distributions and migration routes and/or timing. Historical data from caribou monitoring (since 1970) will be included, where and when possible, in the analyses to advance the development of methodology.

Field Methods

Preparation and Equipment Setup

A number of procurement and regulatory steps will be taken in advance of caribou monitoring efforts. Radio frequencies for radiocollars will be cleared through the National Wildlife Telemetry Frequency Management Database, and the NPS's Regional Radio Coordinator. Because radiocollars must be obtained on the desired frequencies, there can be a several month time lag in the construction of collars. Alternatively, funds can be transferred to the ADFG so that they can purchase collars on the State of Alaska's frequency band, provided acceptable agreements are in place. A complete list of capture and monitoring equipment and a list of suppliers can be found in the Techniques for Caribou Capture and Tagging SOP. Appropriate training and Personal Protective Equipment (PPE) for fixed-wing and helicopter special-use flights must be obtained for field workers.

All aircraft and pilots must be carded for the mission and procured according to NPS, USDI's Aviation Management Directorate (AMD), and USDI Interagency Helicopter Operations Guide (IHOG) regulations. Animal handling personnel must become certified for the Aerial Capture, Eradication and Tagging of Animals (ACETA), as well as obtaining appropriate training in animal anesthesia and handling techniques and aircraft safety. Flight plans and flight following according to Federal Aviation Administration (FAA) and NPS regulations are important for safe operations. Clothing and equipment specifications are determined by NPS ACETA and IHOG guidelines. Permits for animal capture will be obtained from the ADFG, if needed. Capture operations will also get NPS Institutional Animal Care and Use Committee (IACUC) approval. Monitoring staff must perform internal and inter-agency scoping to assure that the project meets National Environmental Policy Act (NEPA) requirements.

Location, Capture, Radio-Tagging of Caribou

Typically, caribou capture operations at Onion Portage involves two or three motorboats working together. Caribou swim across the Kobuk River on their fall migration. Personnel lay in wait until the migrating caribou are in water deep enough to hand capture them from the boats. A series of standard measurements and specimens are collected from each caribou, a radio collar attached, and the caribou is released. Details of caribou capture and handling are described in the Techniques for Caribou Capture and Tagging SOP. If hand capturing at Onion Portage is not possible, net gunning procedures may be utilized.

Collection of Caribou Location Data and Radiotracking

The bulk of caribou location data will be collected remotely via GPS technology integrated into the radiocollars. The data is sent from the collars to ARGOS satellites and then transmitted back to the satellite company and transferred to the NPS. Techniques for processing these data are outlined in the Handling GPS/ARGOS Location Data SOP. Collared caribou are located from fixed-wing aircraft approximately twice per year. Details of equipment needs and radio tracking techniques are found in the Techniques for Radiotracking of Collared Caribou SOP.

Data Management

Overview

This section presents an overview of basic data management procedures for the Arctic Network (ARCN) caribou monitoring vital sign. Refer to standard operating procedures for detailed information on carrying out specific data management tasks.

Overview of Work Flow and Data Products

The caribou monitoring program will deliver 10 major data products (Figure and Table 1) in addition to Natural Resource Data Series reports and Natural Resource Technical Reports. These products correspond to major steps in the caribou monitoring work flow. Each data product is defined by a standard operating procedure and is assigned to an individual with a delivery date. Refer to the standard operating procedures included with this protocol for details.

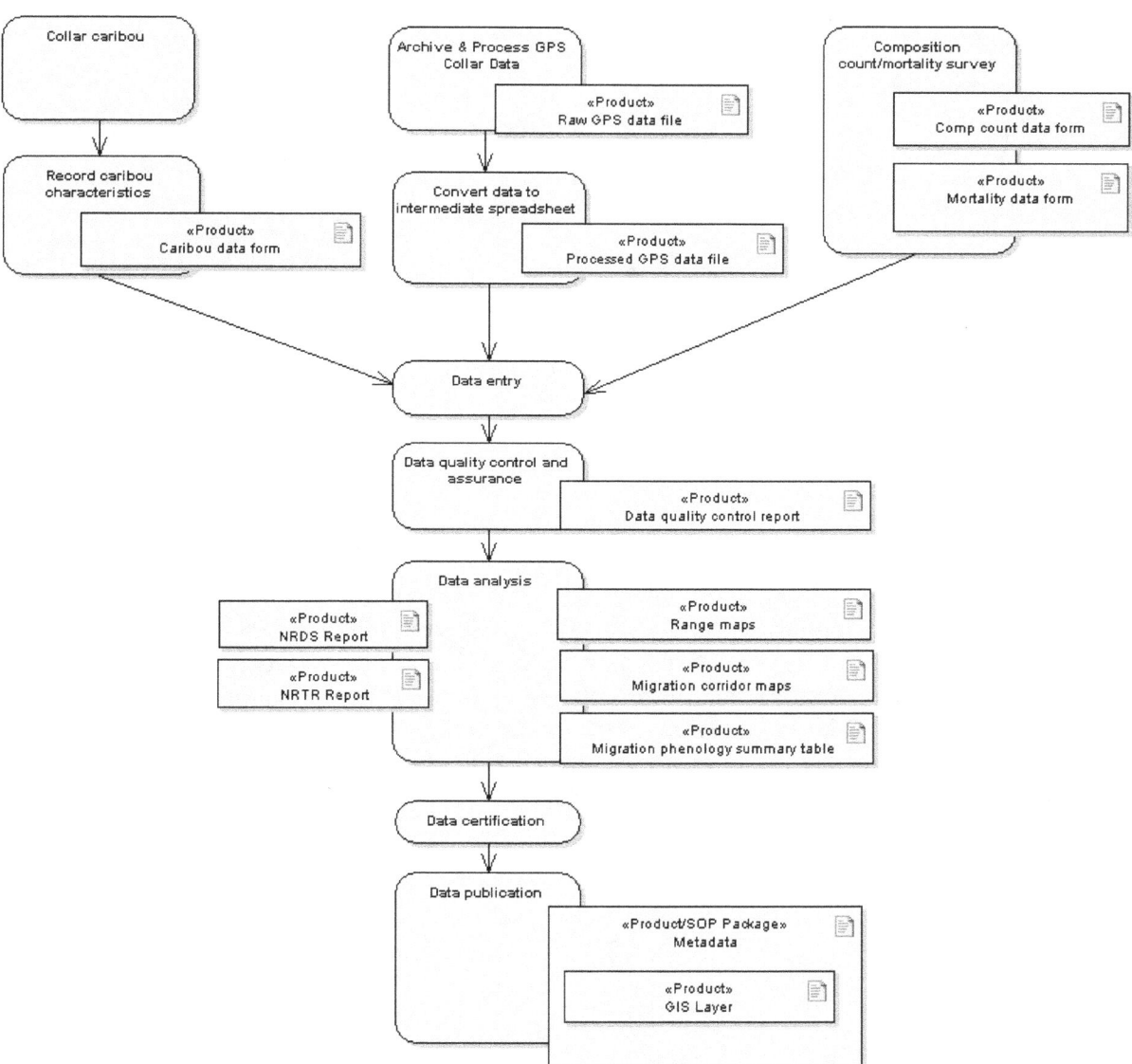

Figure 2. Caribou monitoring work flow showing data products and standard operating procedures.

Table 1. Product delivery schedule, specifications, responsibility and standard operating procedures.

	Deliverable	Format	Schedule	Responsibility	SOP
1	Car bou Capture data form	Paper/PDF	As required	PI	SOP 01: Techniques for Capturing and Tagging Adult Caribou
2	Raw GPS data files	Text file	Weekly	PI	SOP 3: Handling GPS/ARGOS Location Data
3	Processed GPS data files	Spreadsheet	Weekly	PI,DM, Biotech	SOP 3: Handling GPS/ARGOS Location Data
4	Composition count data form			PI,DM, Biotech	SOP 2: Techniques for Radiotracking of Collared Car bou
5	Mortality data form	Paper/PDF		PI,DM, Biotech	SOP 2: Techniques for Radiotracking of Collared Car bou
6	Data quality control report			DM	Standard Operating Prodedure 5: Generating GPS Data Quality Report
7	Range map			PI, Biotech	SOP 4: Data Analysis, Estimating Caribou Seasonal Ranges, Migration Patterns and Survivorship from GPS Data
8	Migration corridor map			PI, Biotech	SOP 4: Data Analysis, Estimating Caribou Seasonal Ranges, Migration Patterns and Survivorship from GPS Data
9	Migration phenology summary table			PI, Biotech	SOP 4: Data Analysis, Estimating Caribou Seasonal Ranges, Migration Patterns and Survivorship from GPS Data
10	Published GIS Layer	Shapefile	Annual	DM	SOP 10: Exporting Data for Publication
	Metadata	FGDC Metadata file (xml)	Annual	DM	SOP 11: Generating Metadata for Data Publication

Data Management Architecture, Application and Database Design

The caribou monitoring data management system is built on a two-tier model consisting of a single client-server back-end database (Microsoft SQL Server 2008 R2) serving multiple front-end applications (Figure , Microsoft Access 2007, ESRI ArcGIS 10). Data entry, quality control and quality assurance operations occur primarily using the Access application while data analysis is done using ArcGIS. Other applications can connect to the database as needed through ODBC connections to the database. The database is situated behind the NPS firewall and access is limited to NPS staff with appropriate permissions.

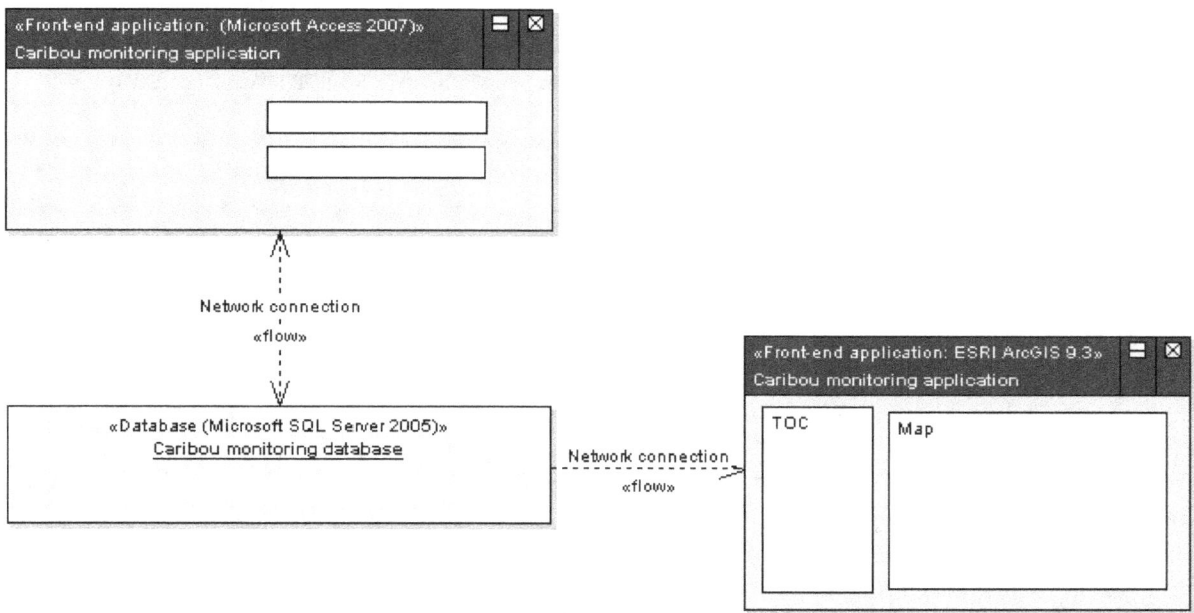

Figure 3. Caribou monitoring data management architecture. The system is a two-tier architecture with client-server database and multiple front-end applications.

Historically, all caribou location data from the WAH was entered and maintained by the ADFG. Some of these data are being consolidated and integrated into databases for storage by the NPS. All location data from GPS collars, capture related data, survival data, and data from radio tracking flights will be maintained in a Microsoft SQL Server 2008 database by the NPS. Caribou monitoring databases have been developed in accordance with the Arctic Network's Data Management Plan.

Database Administration

Database administration will be carried out by the Network data manager, assistant data managers or one or more data managers from other Networks. At no time will there be less than two individuals with 'db_owner' privileges. Accommodation must be made during periods of absence for these individuals. Administration tasks are specifically addressed in the data management SOPs included with this protocol as well as available through Microsoft SQL Server 2008 documentation.

Data Acquisition and Processing

All aspects of data management, including data entry and editing, data verification, quality assurance and control procedures are described in the Network data management plan as well as the data management standard operating procedures included with this protocol.

Data Development, Delivery and Review

Data archival will be done in concert with data certification. Data certification columns exist in the database which will be filled in appropriately to distinguish new or raw data that has not undergone quality assurance procedures from certified or 'finished' data. All data will be archived within our SQL Server database and within our database backup files. Database 'snapshots' may be archived on the Natural Resource Information Portal. Data will be disseminated to the Western Arctic Caribou Herd Working Group annually. Data may not be shared further than this group except according to the conditional use statement found in Appendix 5.

Analysis and Reporting

Determining Caribou Distribution, Migration Patterns, and Survivorship

Caribou distribution will be determined using GPS location data transmitted via satellite telemetry. A home range program (e.g., Rodgers et al. 2007) will be used to generate 50% and 95% utilization distribution polygons using fixed kernel analyses (Seaman and Powell 1996) for each season (calving, insect relief, summer, and winter). These seasons will be defined using predefined dates (Russell et al., 1993, Dau 2007, Person et al. 2007) and the movement rates of the caribou themselves. Timing and location of migration of individual caribou will be assessed. Characteristics of spring and fall migration that will be quantified include distance to key villages, timing of passing key villages (i.e., Noatak, Selawik and Shungnak), rivers (i.e., Noatak, Selawik and Kobuk) and other physiographic features. Survivorship of caribou will be assessed using a known-fate analysis that accounts for the number of collars deployed (White and Burnham 1999). Details of determining caribou distribution, migration patterns, and survivorship can be found in the Data Analysis Including Estimating Caribou Seasonal Ranges, Migration Patterns and Survivorship from GPS Data SOP (#4).

Monitoring flights will concentrate on visual observations of caribou during early October to assess how they handled the stress of capture (through survivorship, abnormal movement patterns and/or behavior) and environmental conditions. A similar flight will take place in late winter (April). Groups of caribou will be photographed.

Reporting the Results of Caribou Monitoring

Reports generated by the caribou monitoring effort, and the vital signs monitoring program in general, will be promptly produced, appropriate to their target audience, widely available, and visually accessible. Concise summaries will be a part of each report produced. Reports will conform to guidelines set by the Arctic Network and the Alaska Region Inventory and Monitoring Plan. Graphical methods, maps, and other visual aids will be used to make results readily understood.

An annual administrative report and work plan will be produced in the fall of each year. The report will account for the expenditure of funds and FTEs, and describe the objectives, tasks, accomplishments, and products of the monitoring effort during the previous fiscal year. The report is designed to improve communication within each park, the Arctic Network, the Alaska Region, and the National Monitoring Program. Its intended audience includes park superintendents, park natural resource staff, network staff, regional coordinators, and Service wide program managers. The report will be written by the park biologists implementing the caribou monitoring protocol, and reviewed and approved by the Arctic Network, Regional Office and Service-wide Program managers.

An annual report will be prepared for publication each October, reporting on caribou monitoring activities during the previous year (September 1 - August 31). It will contain capture information, seasonal ranges, migration patterns, survivorship and other data. The annual report will provide a summary of all caribou monitoring activities and data for the year, and describe the current condition of the herd. Any changes in monitoring protocols will be documented. The intended audience for the annual report includes park resource managers, network staff, and external scientists. The report will be written by the park biologists implementing the caribou monitoring protocol, and peer-reviewed within the Arctic Network.

In addition to the scheduled annual reports, results of the caribou monitoring effort will be presented at Arctic Network meetings and at other symposia, conferences, and workshops. Caribou monitoring data will be provided to park interpretive staff for written and oral presentation to visitors. Significant findings will be reported in scientific journals and popular publications.

Personnel Requirements and Training

A GAAR wildlife biologist will serve as principal investigator for caribou monitoring for the Arctic Network. Capture efforts will primarily be conducted at Onion Portage in cooperation with biologists from other agencies lead by the ADFG, if possible. Radio tracking efforts will be conducted by AMD certified pilots with wildlife biologists or wildlife technicians as observers, or by pilots alone. When NPS personnel take part in telemetry flights, they must have appropriate aircraft safety training as specified by the AMD, and wear PPE suitable for Special Use flights under AMD guidelines. Personnel needs for caribou monitoring are not great enough to require additional park staff, though a dedicated technician would reduce the data management work load substantially. The greatest need for specialized expertise will come if the need for aerial capture and radio collaring of caribou arises. NPS personnel involved in capture operations must have certification in ACETA, proper training in animal immobilization and handling, and appropriate aircraft safety and management training under IHOG regulations. The selection of aircraft and pilots is of great importance for the safe and economical capture and monitoring of caribou. A project aviation safety plan will be prepared and approved prior to operations.

In addition to park biologists and pilots, important personnel in the caribou monitoring effort include collaborators at the ADFG, BLM, University of Alaska Fairbanks (UAF), USGS, FWS, the Arctic Network data manager, and park GIS specialists for help with data management and analysis.

Operational Requirements

Annual Workload and Field Schedule

Capture operations are usually carried out in early fall (September) as caribou swim across the Kobuk River on their southward migration. The caribou are physically restrained by biologists in motorboats. Adults receive radiocollars and calves are weighed. Additional captures may take place in winter, if necessary, via aerial net gunning when conditions are suitable. Yearlings and/or adults will receive collars; calves will not be radio collared. Radio tracking flights will typically occur in October and April to assess how caribou handled capture (through survivorship, abnormal movement patterns and/or behavior) and/or to document environmental conditions, reproductive status and group size.

Facility and Equipment Needs

No specialized facilities are required for the caribou monitoring effort. Laboratory analyses for non-core objectives, such as genetic and disease screening, will be carried out by cooperators (e.g., UAF, USGS, ADFG) as resources are available. Equipment required for capture and monitoring of caribou is detailed in the Techniques for Caribou Capture and Tagging SOP. A complete kit for field capture of caribou can be expected to cost about $2,500 (2011 prices). Equipment to perform radio tracking from a fixed-wing aircraft totals about $4,000 (2011 prices). At present, adequate field equipment is already present within the Arctic Network. The costs of caribou monitoring lies primarily in satellite data acquisition fees, aircraft costs, and GPS radiocollars.

Startup Costs and Budget Considerations

A caribou monitoring effort can be implemented in the Arctic Network without the need for additional personnel or facilities. Field work, data management and reporting will be handled by existing park staff. Costs estimated in the table below (based on 2011 prices) are for establishing and maintaining a caribou monitoring effort covering 30-45 caribou, but costs will be highly dependent on the mortality of collared caribou.

Estimated Costs	WAH
Satellite download fees	40,000
Annual Collar Costs	35,000
Annual aircraft use budget	15,000
Travel (e.g., WAHWG), supplies, misc.	15,000
Total	**105,000**

Procedure for Revising the Protocol and Archiving Previous Versions of the Protocol

Over time, revisions to both the Protocol Narrative and to specific SOPs are to be expected. Careful documentation of changes to the protocol, and a library of previous protocol versions are essential for maintaining consistency in data collection and for appropriate treatment of the data during data summary and analysis. The caribou monitoring database for each monitoring component contains a field that identifies which version of the protocol was being used when the data were collected.

The rationale for dividing a sampling protocol into a Protocol Narrative with supporting SOPs is based on the following:

- The Protocol Narrative is a general overview of the protocol that gives the history and justification for doing the work and an overview of the sampling methods, but that does not provide all of the methodological details. The Protocol Narrative will only be revised if major changes are made to the protocol.
- The SOPs, in contrast, are very specific step-by-step instructions for performing a given task. They are expected to be revised more frequently than the protocol narrative.
- When a SOP is revised, in most cases, it is not necessary to revise the Protocol Narrative to reflect the specific changes made to the SOP.
- All versions of the Protocol Narrative and SOPs will be archived in a Protocol Library.

The steps for changing the protocol (either the Protocol Narrative or the SOPs) are outlined in the Revising the Protocol SOP. Each SOP contains a Revision History Log that should be filled out each time a SOP is revised to explain why the change was made, and to assign a new Version Number to the revised SOP. The new version of the SOP and/or Protocol Narrative should then be archived in the I&M Protocol Library under the appropriate folder.

References

Dau, J. 2007. Units 21D, 22A, 22B, 22C, 22D, 22E, 23, 24 and 26A caribou management report. Pages 174-231 in P. Harper, editor. Caribou management report of survey and inventory activities 1 July 2004-30 June 2006. Alaska Department of Fish and Game. Project 3.0. Juneau, AK.

Davis J.L., Valkenburg P., and Reynolds H.V. 1980. Population dynamics of Alaska's Western Arctic Caribou Herd. Proceedings of the International Reindeer/Caribou Symposium 2:595-604.

Murie, O. 1935. Alaska-Yukon caribou. North American Fauna 54. US Department of Agriculture, Bureau of Biological Survey, Washington DC.

Person, B. T., A. K. Prichard, G. M. Carroll, D. A. Yokel, R. S. Suydam and J. C. George. 2007. Distribution and movements of the Teshekpuk Caribou Herd 1990-2005: prior to oil and gas development. Arctic 60:238-250.

Rodgers, A.R., A.P. Carr, H.L. Beyer, L. Smith, and J.G. Kie. 2007. HRT: Home Range Tools for ArcGIS. Ontario Ministry of Natural Resources, Centre for Northern Forest Ecosystem Research, Thunder Bay, Ontario, Canada.

Russell, D. E., A. M. Martell, and W. A. C. Nixon. 1993. Range ecology of the Porcupine Caribou Herd in Canada. Rangifer Special Issue 8:1-167.

Skoog, R.O. 1968. Ecology of caribou in Alaska. Ph. D. Diss., Univ. California-Berkley. 699 pp.

U. S. Congress, 1980. Alaska National Interest Lands Conservation Act, PUBLIC LAW 96-487-DEC. 2, 1980. 94 STAT. 2371. http://www.r7.fws.gov/asm/anilca/toc.html

U. S. Department of the Interior. 1988. Interagency Helicopter Operations Guide. NFES 1885. National Interagency Fire Center, Boise ID.

U. S. Department of the Interior. 1994. Aerial Capture, Eradication and Tagging of Animals (ACETA) Handbook. Departmental Manual 351 DM 2 - 351 DM 3. 8 pp. Office of Aircraft Services, USDI. http://www.oas.gov/library/dm/acetahb.pdf.

Western Arctic Caribou Herd Working Group. 2003. Western Arctic Caribou Herd Cooperative Management Plan. 33 pp.

Standard Operating Procedure 1: Techniques for Capturing and Tagging Adult Caribou

Version 1.0 August, 2012, K. Joly

Revision History Log:

Prev. Version #	Revision Date	Author	Changes Made	Reason for Change	New Version #

Scope and Application

This SOP explains the process for locating, capturing and tagging caribou for radio-telemetry monitoring. This SOP also describes the measurements and specimens that are collected from captured caribou, and the disposition of specimens. The steps for changing the protocol are outlined in the Revising the Protocol SOP.

Preparation and Equipment Procurement

Once it has been decided to implement a caribou monitoring program, a number of procurement and regulatory steps must be taken, well in advance of any capture efforts. Radio frequencies for radiocollars must be cleared through the National Wildlife Telemetry Frequency Management Database, and the NPS's Regional Radio Coordinator. Approved frequencies will be spaced at least 10 kilohertz apart. Because radiocollars must be obtained on the desired frequencies, there can be a time lag of several months or more in the construction of collars. Similar time lags exist if funds are transferred to ADFG to purchase collars on Alaska State-band frequencies using acceptable terms of contracting. Minimum equipment for a caribou monitoring study should include radiocollars, at least one telemetry receiver, antennae, radio telemetry receiver cables, wing strut brackets for telemetry antennae, and a switchbox for aerial telemetry. In addition, for caribou capture, a net gun, nets, and a well-stocked capture kit are required (Appendix 1).

Appropriate PPE for fixed-wing and helicopter special-use flights must be obtained for field workers. Permits for animal capture will be obtained from the ADFG, as needed. Personnel will have appropriate ACETA training for aerial capture work. Monitoring staff will perform internal and inter-agency scoping to assure that the project meets National Environmental Policy Act requirements.

Caribou Capture and Aerial Tracking

Procedures
Choosing a study area.
The WAH was chosen to be the monitored caribou herd because it is the only herd which regularly utilizes all 5 Arctic Network park units. The caribou themselves will determine the actual study area.

Timing and logistics of capture work.
Most caribou capture efforts will take place in September at Onion Portage on the Kobuk River within KOVA. These operations have historically been led by the ADFG. The collaborators travel to Ambler in a chartered plane and travel down the Kobuk River in motorboats to Onion Portage. The NPS' Giddings' cabin is used as a support facility for the capture operations.

Netting of caribou may be necessary if capture operations at Onion Portage are not sufficient to meet the objectives of this protocol. Net gunning may be considered if the capture sample size from Onion Portage is small or if distribution of collars needs to occur over a wider area, and/or if sub-populations are identified that do not utilize Onion Portage (e.g., subpopulations or resident caribou in BELA). The timing of netting operations will depend on the seasonal distribution of WAH and surface and weather conditions. The NPS will take the lead role in netting operations with assistance from cooperating agencies (ADFG, BLM, and/or FWS) as appropriate.

Because of the increased difficulty and danger of field work at extremely low temperatures, capture operations will not be attempted at temperatures lower than -30° F (-34° C). A helicopter and helicopter pilot approved and carded by AMD for animal capture work will be scheduled, and fixed-wing tracking aircraft will be scheduled to locate caribou for capture. All aircraft and pilots must be approved for the mission and procured according to NPS, AMD, and IHOG regulations. Approved flight plans and flight following outlined in FAA and NPS regulations are important for safe operations. Clothing and equipment specifications as determined by NPS ACETA and IHOG guidelines will be followed. Radio communication for flight plans, flight following, and communication between the various aircraft involved in the capture operation will follow the aviation policies of Western Arctic Parklands (WEAR) and GAAR.

Aerial tracking.
Aerial tracking will be conducted in October and April. Tracking is best performed from small, slow-flying aircraft such as the Piper PA-18 Supercub. However, the herd can be in very remote areas during these times of the year and it may be more efficient and economical to use a larger aircraft such as a Cessna 185. If possible, the observer will record if the collared caribou has a calf present. Latitude, longitude, group size and habitat will also be recorded for each collared caribou. For more details, see the Techniques for Radiotracking of Collared Caribou SOP (SOP #2).

Caribou Handling and Specimen Collection

Procedures

1. *Physical Restraint of Swimming Caribou at Onion Portage*. Capture crews wait on the south bank for caribou to appear on the north bank of the Kobuk River and start across the river. They then use motorboats to get close to caribou swimming across the river and physically restrain them while the caribou is in water deep enough that they cannot touch bottom. If the caribou can touch bottom, they should be released immediately before they inflict damage to themselves and/or people in the boats. For the capture of bulls, a second boat parallels the first to create a chute in which the bull can be restrained by biologists in both boats. In the case of cows, a second boat will capture its calf, if present. For both bulls and cows a blood sample is obtained, a small hair sample can be removed, and they are radiocollared and receive a qualitative assessment of body condition all while in deep water. The blood sample is used for disease screening and archiving. The hair sample may be utilized in DNA analyses. If present, the calf is sexed, brought into the boat and weighed. If feasible, the jaw lengths of calves will be determined. Cow and calf pairs are release at the same time and efforts are made to see that they are reunited on the far bank of the river. Blood samples, results of individual blood tests, body condition scores, as well sex and weights of calves are all currently maintained by the ADFG; the NPS will work on collaborating with ADFG to share these data with all of the cooperating agencies. Summary results are available to the general public.

2. *Net gunning from helicopters.* Caribou are captured by netting with a Coda Netgun® (Coda Netguns, Mesa, AZ). The net is deployed by four weights tied at the corners of the net. The weights are propelled with a .308 caliber blank charge loaded into the breech of the gun behind the net. During capture operations, loaded nets are deployed and stored in fiberglass canisters. The gunner is situated immediately behind the pilot. Communication between pilot and gunner requires a 'voice activated' microphone. During capture operations, the gunner's door is removed. The gunner is held in the helicopter by a shooting harness while he/she leans out the door to fire the net gun. The pilot maneuvers the helicopter to match the speed of the fleeing caribou, usually within 10 meters of the animal. The gunner fires a net over the caribou. The caribou runs into the net and becomes ensnared. The relatively small size, speed and maneuverability of caribou make them difficult targets, and pilot and shooter experience are necessary for successful and safe capture. The most common cause of death among netted caribou is broken necks or legs that occur when the animal is tripped up at full speed. Another mechanism of injury is from the weighs on the corners of the net striking the caribou. Caribou that are seriously injured (e.g., broken leg) during capture operations will be euthanized with a firearm. When a caribou has been successfully netted, the helicopter will move in to drop off a mugger who will hobble and blindfold the caribou.

Care must be taken in selecting the area where caribou are netted. Steep terrain and open water present hazards for the animal and for handling personnel, and availability of helicopter landing areas can determine the distance that handling personnel must travel to the netted animal. Careful monitoring of caribou by spotter planes, along with monitoring and judicious herding by the helicopter, can create or maintain safe conditions for the caribou and capture personnel and increase the efficiency of the operation. A caribou that continues to struggle after being blindfolded and hobbled may require the administration of a sedative. Personnel administering drugs to caribou and handling drugged caribou should have current certification under the NPS ACETA program, as well as training in wildlife chemical immobilization. The presence of a veterinarian during capture operations is desirable but not necessary.

A. *Initial evaluation and body temperature check.* A netted caribou should be approached with caution but quickly to reduce the potential for injury. If the caribou has been netted on uneven ground, or in an awkward position, it should be repositioned to a flat spot and laid either on its side or on its sternum (preferable). Verification that the airway is clear and the caribou is breathing should be done immediately.

Upon reaching a netted caribou, handlers should physically restrain the animal, and cover its eyes with a blindfold which should protect them from sunlight, foreign objects, and drying. Antibiotic eye ointment should be applied to each eye. Once the animal has been blindfolded, the handlers can then hobble together 3 - 4 legs.

One of the more dangerous complications of netting, besides capture related injury, is hyperthermia (overheating) caused by the exertion and stress of capture. Among the first actions to be performed on a netted caribou, therefore, is taking body temperature. A battery-powered, digital thermometer commonly available for human use is adequate for monitoring the body temperature of captured caribou. LCD readouts may become sluggish or inoperative in very cold weather, so spare thermometers, including an older-style analog fever thermometer, should be carried. Temperature is taken rectally, with a thermometer or probe lubricated with K-Y Jelly® and inserted at least two inches to obtain core body temperature. Normal body temperature for caribou is about 101° F (38.3° C). If the observed temperature is greater than 104° F (40° C), attempts should be made to cool the caribou by packing the groin area with snow or placing the caribou in a sternally recumbent position with its underside exposed to the snow. If body temperature continues to climb, the caribou should be immediately released.

B. *Vital signs monitoring.* It is important to evaluate the status of a netted animal by monitoring its vital signs; particularly temperature, pulse, and respiration. Most importantly, handlers should immediately verify that the airway is clear and an animal is breathing when it is first handled. Second in importance is verification that body temperature stays in the desirable range of 98-104 ° F (36.7-40° C). These are not absolute thresholds, but an animal whose body temperature is approaching the limits of this range should be treated pre-emptively, particularly if serial temperature measurements have shown a trend toward hyperthermia or hypothermia. Capillary refill time, an index of cardiac function, can be measured by pressing on a non-pigmented part of the gum, releasing pressure, and determining the time to restoration of color. A capillary refill time of less than 2 seconds generally implies adequate blood pressure. A slower refill time indicates low blood pressure or other circulatory dysfunction. All vital signs, along with any booster drugs or other drugs administered, should be recorded along with the time (military or 2400 hour time) on the table provided on the capture sheet (Appendix 2).

C. *General condition and appearance.* The general body condition of captured caribou should be briefly described. A caribou in good condition should have a layer of fat over the pelvis,

18

ribs, and spine making them palpable but not sharply so. On a caribou in excellent condition (score of 5), the pelvis ribs and spine may not be felt beneath a heavy layer of fat. Caribou in fair condition, and poor condition, will show decreasing fat levels and more sharply palpable bones. Condition should be recorded on the data sheet.

Netted caribou should be examined for old or new injuries, including broken bones, abrasions, and abnormalities of the skin and fur. Digital photographs should be taken of any injuries or abnormalities. New or old wounds should be treated with the application of Nolvasan® antibiotic ointment or nitrofurazone spray. Injured caribou may be given a long-lasting antibiotic such as Flo-Cillin® or Dual-Cillin®, with a concentration of 150,000 units per ml, at a dose of 1.5 ml per 10 kg of body weight, administered subcutaneously. A total of 10 ml per typically-sized adult female should be sufficient.

D. *Body measurements.* Caribou should be weighed on an accurate scale with units (pounds or kilograms) recorded as needed. Handlers should use a weighing net and suspend it from the scale at the top of a weigh pole. The data sheet contains spaces for recording body length (tip of nose to base of tail), neck circumference, jaw, metatarsus and hindfoot lengths, and chest girth (distance around the chest immediately behind the front legs). These measurements should be taken in centimeters with a cloth measuring tape or calipers. Although many other measurements may be taken, speed and efficiency of handling argue for maintaining this brief set. The most valuable measurements for long-term evaluation of morphological change are likely to be measurements of the jaw, metatarsus and hindfoot lengths. Please see CARMA's Level 2 Monitoring Protocols for diagrams and photos that depict how to collect these data. These procedures can be found at /arcn/monitoring/vital signs/caribou/protocols/supportinginfo/CARMA level2_body_condition.pdf or on CARMA's webpage (http://carmanetwork.onconfluence.com/display/public/home).

E. *Identification, collaring and tagging.* Each captured caribou is assigned a unique number, based on the year and the order in which it was captured. Thus, the first caribou captured in 2009 will be named 0901. Preceding this with the species and herd, as in CARIBOU WAH 0901, should provide a unique identifier even when data or specimens from many areas are combined. Capture date should be recorded in the format month/day/year. A general description of the caribou's capture location (distance from some landmark) is recorded, along with the latitude and longitude of the capture site in degrees, minutes, and decimal minutes (datum WGS84). The sex and age of the caribou are recorded. For adult caribou, an estimated age in years should be recorded.

The standard radiocollar used for monitoring will be the Telonics TGW-4680 collar. The frequency and serial number of the collar are recorded on the data sheet. The magnet, taped to the collar to keep it from broadcasting, is removed to start radio transmission. A telemetry receiver is used to verify the operation and frequency of the collar before it is deployed on a caribou. Collars are affixed snugly around a caribou's neck, leaving enough room to insert a hand between the collar and the neck. A collar should be tight enough that it does not flop around excessively when the animal moves. Collars placed on yearling or young caribou should be left an inch or two looser to allow for growth. Belting material that extends beyond the collar attachment should be trimmed off but care must be taken not to cut the antenna off when the belting is trimmed away. Before capture efforts begin, each collar should be labeled with a waterproof marker with the radio frequency and serial number. A nut driver for tightening nuts and sheet metal shears for cutting collar material are needed.

Caribou will be collared with GPS/ARGOS collars, which determine an animal's location using the GPS satellite system, and data will be uploaded through the ARGOS satellite system. The collars will be programmed to take three GPS location per day. The lifespan of these collars is expected to be approximately 3-4 years. Each GPS collar carries a duty cycled conventional VHS transmitter so that it may also be tracked from aircraft. Specifications for GPS collars currently being used are given in Appendix 3.

F. *Reproductive evaluation.* Presence of calf should be recorded on the datasheet during capture as well as if the cow is currently lactating.

G. *Specimen collection.* Blood is drawn from the cephalic (foreleg) vein, using either a large (35 ml) syringe with an 18 gauge needle, or a Vac-U-Tainer® system (Becton, Dickinson Inc). For disease antibody screening, whole blood is placed in two serum separation tubes (red and gray stopper) for subsequent centrifugation, freezing and analysis. Tubes containing EDTA anticoagulant (purple stoppers) are used to store blood for hematology and genetic analysis. All blood tubes should be gently upended several times to mix the contents.

In cold weather, blood samples must be kept from freezing, which causes cell destruction. Tubes should be labeled with the animal number and stored in a protected location (e.g., a cooler with a hot water bottle or hand warmer in it to prevent freezing) until returning from the field.

In addition to collecting blood, we may collect other specimens for genetic analysis. These samples may include buccal swabs (cotton swab rubbed on the lining of the mouth), and a tuft of hairs with roots attached. These samples will be placed in small manila envelopes for storage. Fecal pellets for dietary analysis may also be collected. These will be stored in plastic whirl packs. Care must be taken to label all specimens with the animal number, because multiple caribou are typically captured in a day. A tooth may be extracted using a tooth elevator for cementum aging. Lydacaine or similar anesthetic may be used to numb the gum.

It is convenient to prepare specimen collection packs in ziplock bags, with the supplies needed for one caribou. These might include one 35 ml syringe for blood drawing, two 6ml or 10 ml syringes for penicillin dispension, several 18 gauge (green) needles 1.5 inch in length, two 10 ml serum separation tubes, two 10 ml blood tube ("red top") containing Longmire's Solution, two 3 ml EDTA (purple top) tubes, and several small manila envelopes for tissue specimens.

H. *Recovery of netted caribou.* There is no recovery time for netted caribou. Once released, the caribou should be able to travel under its own power immediately.

I. *Personnel, photos, remarks.* Fields on the data sheet allow the recording of the names of the capture crew, a record of photographs taken, and other remarks. The remarks section can be used to record any injuries or abnormalities not noted elsewhere on the data sheet, unusual coat color or physical conformation, identity and activity of other caribou during the capture operation, other caribou captured at the same time, significant weather conditions, the condition of the caribou on release, and any other observations that may be useful in interpreting laboratory results or the subsequent behavior of the caribou.

J. *Specimen handling and disposition.* When capture personnel return to the laboratory, serum separation tubes are centrifuged for 15 minutes, and the serum poured into screw-topped plastic CryoTubes® (Nalge Nunc Inernational) and frozen. The original blood collection tube is discarded, but the plug of cellular material in it (blood clot) is kept as a genetic sample. Whole blood in Longmire buffer collected for genetic analyses is subdivided into several CryoTubes and frozen. Hair and buccal swab specimens, also collected for genetic analysis, are stored in manila envelopes at room temperature. Both blood and tissue samples are collected to ensure quality DNA extraction. EDTA (purple-topped) tubes are stored in a refrigerator, not frozen, if they will be used for hematology analysis (e.g., a caribou with an apparent infection). This will be done periodically (3-5 years). Otherwise, blood from EDTA tubes can be transferred to unbreakable CryoTubes and frozen for a genetic specimen. The final containers for all specimens are labeled in permanent marker, both on the caps and sides of each tube, with the species, herd, park unit, animal number, capture date, sex, , and tissue type (whole blood, blood clot, serum, hair, or tissue, etc.).

None of the specimens collected require rapid handling or express shipping. Genetic specimens may be sent to the USGS Alaska Science Center Molecular Ecology Laboratory in Anchorage. Samples will be sub-sampled by NPS and deposited at various agencies. Redundancy of specimens will allow long- term storage by USGS, ADFG, and the University of Alaska Museum Frozen Tissue Collection, so that archival specimens are available for future analyses. Frozen serum specimens will be sent to the ADFG for disease analysis. In cases where a systemic infection or other blood abnormality is suspected, hematology analysis of whole blood preserved in EDTA will be performed by a veterinary laboratory.

K. *Daily equipment maintenance*. At the end of the day, processing kits should be cleaned out and dried, refuse disposed of and contents replenished. Capture guns are cleaned, and nets are cleaned and allowed to air dry. Data sheets are checked for completeness, photocopied (if possible) and stored securely.

L. *Human safety and legal issues.* Human safety should have the highest priority in conducting animal capture operations. Many aircraft safety issues are mitigated by adherence to the IHOG guidelines for helicopter operation, including training in aviation safety and the use of appropriate PPE for special-use helicopter operations. An exemption, arranged between NPS and AMD, allows deviation from some PPE specifications, recognizing the importance of appropriate clothing for survival in Alaska. Thus, all-leather shoes need not be worn for flying. Nevertheless, survival in an aircraft accident will be maximized by the avoidance of synthetic fabrics and the selection of Nomex®, Kevlar®, wool or cotton clothing.

Selection of capable, experienced pilots is perhaps the most important safety consideration in caribou capture work. Caribou capture involves mountain flying and low-level operations, often in cold weather, and requires skills that not only require a great deal of experience to perfect, but also require innate abilities that are not necessarily teachable. As long as a pool of experienced pilots is available in Alaska, and they are available under AMD and NPS procurement guidelines, they should be used for this work. Attempting to locate and capture caribou with inexperienced pilots is likely to substantially increase the cost of the operation, and cause increased risk to pilots and crew.

Safe handling of capture equipment and drugs is ensured by thorough training in ACETA procedures and wildlife immobilization techniques. The use of dart rifles, rather than net guns, for caribou capture allows capture in a greater variety of conditions (vegetation and/or terrain). However, caribou are harvested year round and thus net guns are the preferred option to avoid the possibility of a hunter consuming a drug tainted caribou. Careful, deliberate attention to the details of safe aircraft and firearms operation are required for safe wildlife capture. The consequences of a net fired into the rotor could be fatal.

Radio communications are an important safety factor in this and all aircraft operations. Filing and closing flight plans with FAA, obtaining weather reports, flight following with park dispatch, and most importantly, coordination between the various aircraft involved in the operation, are all accomplished with appropriate radio equipment. Radio equipment for aircraft is specified under the contracts and rental agreements with AMD. Handheld radios, both on aircraft and NPS frequencies, should be carried by personnel on the ground so that they can communicate with aircraft and with park dispatch. Radio frequencies for coordination between aircraft are arranged at the beginning of the operation.

Other hazards that may be associated with caribou capture include extreme weather conditions (causing danger of frostbite, hypothermia, and increased chance of injury from tools and other equipment), terrain hazards including falls and avalanche danger, and injuries sustained while lifting and moving caribou. These dangers can be mitigated by suspending capture operations when weather is too harsh, by avoiding caribou capture in overly steep terrain, by wearing proper clothing, and by thoughtful behavior even when circumstances are rushed or stressful.

M. *Data management*. The attached caribou capture data sheet should be printed on Rite-in the Rain® paper. Graphite pencils should be used to record data. The data sheet should be examined before leaving a recovering animal, to check for measurements or observations that may have been missed. If enough personnel are present, designating one person to record data can facilitate the consistency and accuracy of the process. This is especially true when more than one caribou is being processed together. The capture location should be waypointed with a GPS unit, and the coordinates recorded on the data sheet as soon as practical.

Caribou capture data will be entered and stored in the designated Caribou Monitoring Database and Application as described in the Data Management SOP. Details of data management for long-term caribou monitoring are also contained in the Data Management SOP.

Addresses and Contact Information

Genetic analysis: Dr. Sandra Talbot   (907) 786-7188
USGS/BRD Alaska Science Center
Molecular Ecology laboratory
4230 University Drive Suite 201
Anchorage, AK 99508-4650
http://www.absc.usgs.gov/research/programs/technical.htm#genetics

Caribou necropsy   Dr. Kimberlee Beckmen, DVM   (907) 459-7257

ACETA Training   Institute of Arctic Biology
Room 311 Irving I Building
P.O. box 757000
University of Alaska, Fairbanks
Fairbanks, AK 99775-7000
http://www.uaf.edu/iacuc/vet/

Telemetry Equipment: Telonics, Inc.   (602) 892-4444
932 E. Impala Ave.
Mesa, AZ 85204-6699
www.telonics.com

Advanced Telemetry Systems   (763) 444-9267
470 First Avenue North
Box 398
Isanti, MN 55040
www.atstrack.com

Communications Specialists Inc.   (800) 854-0547
426 West Taft Ave.
Orange, California 92865-4224
http://www.com-spec.com/r1000/r1000.htm

Capture Equipment   Nasco - Modesto   (800) 558 -595
4825 Stoddard Road
P.O. Box 3837
Modesto, California 95352-3837

Flight suits, PPE   Gibson & Barnes   (800) 440-5904
1675 Pioneer Way
El Cajon, CA 92020
www.flightsuits.com

Aircraft Procurement   USDI Aviation Management Directorate   (907) 271-3700

& Aircraft Safety Training	4405 Lear Court Anchorage, AK 99502-1032 http://amd.nbc.gov	
Syringes, medical supplies	Alaska Scientific 664 East Dowling Road Anchorage, AK 99518 http://www.alaskascientific.net/	(907) 563-2758

References

U. S. Department of the Interior. 1988. Interagency Helicopter Operations Guide. NFES 1885. National Interagency Fire Center, Boise ID.

U. S. Department of the Interior. 1994. Aerial Capture, Eradication and Tagging of Animals (ACETA) Handbook. Departmental Manual 351 DM 2 - 351 DM 3. 8 pp. Office of Aircraft Services, USDI. http://www.oas.gov/library/dm/acetahb.pdf.

Appendix 1: Recommended Equipment List (2011 prices)

Radiocollars, GPS/ARGOS (Telonics) TGW-4680	2850.00
Telemetry receiver (Advanced Telemetry Systems)	
Model R4000 (4 Megahertz frequency range) _or_	2750.00
Model R8000 (8 Megahertz frequency range)	(3150.00)
Telemetry receiver (Communications Specialists)	
R-1000 Telemetry Receiver (handheld scanner)	695.00
Aircraft tracking antenna, RA-2A (Telonics) (pair)	220.00
Aircraft antenna brackets, TAB-3 (Telonics) (pair)	540.00
Antenna cables, 17 foot (Telonics) (pair)	70.00
Antenna switchbox (Advanced Telemetry Systems)	95.00
Antenna switchbox (TAC-2, Telonics)	125.00
3-element folding handheld antenna (Advanced Telemetry Systems)	120.00
2-element flexible (rubber ducky) antenna (RA-14K, Telonics)	212.00
Net Gun	350.00
Blank charges	12.00
Nets (minimum of 3 10'x10')	23.00
Shooting harness for helicopter	100.00
Nut driver for collar bolts	5.00
Sheet metal shears for cutting collars	10.00
Calipers (metric vernier, stainless or plastic)	20.00
Tape measure (inches and centimeters)	5.00
Plastic tackle box for capture equipment	20.00
Scale, Pesola, 300 kg capacity, 1 kg accuracy	200.00
Net and carabineers for weighing	100.00
Blindfold	10.00
Backpack for capture gear	50.00
Small sharps container	10.00
Digital and/or analog fever thermometer	20.00
35 ml syringes, Luer Lock, (Monoject brand), case of 200	200.00
18 gauge needles, (green) Luer-Lock, 1 inch length, package of 100	12.00
Vacutainer® serum separation tubes (red/gray tops), 9.5 ml draw, package of 100	50.00
Empty vacutainer tubes, (red tops)10 ml draw, package of 100	25.00
EDTA blood collection tubes (purple top), 3 ml draw, package of 100	25.00
NUNC^{TM} CryoTube® Vials, 2 ml, self standing, screw top, model 375418 (450 pack)	175.00
Flo-Cillin, 100 ml vial	20.00
Sterile Water, 30 ml vial	3.00@
Nolvasan antibiotic ointment, 7 oz jar	20.00
Nitrofurazone antibiotic spray, 7 oz spray bottle	10.00
Centrifuge	400.00
Small manila envelopes	10.00
Surgical gloves	5.00
Disinfectant wipes	5.00

Appendix 2: Caribou Capture Data Sheet

A. Onion Portage (Physical Restraint while Swimming)

WAH Caribou			Capture - Onion Portage 2009							Page 1 of _____		Revised 7/27/2009
										Observer: _____		
Capture #	Date	ID	Freq	Time	Sex	Blood Sample?	Hair Sample?	with calf?	calf sex	calf weight (kg)	calf jaw (cm)	Comment
1	9/12	09-01	148.740	13:12	F	Y	Y	Y	M	55.2	21	1 antler (L)
2	9/12	09-02	149.230	13:16	F	Y	Y	N				Fat
3	9/12	09-25	149.650	13:33	F	Y	Y	Y	F	45.7	19	limping
4												
5												
6												
7												
8												
9												
10												
11												
12												
13												

B. Net gunning via helicopter

Caribou Capture Form – WAH Fall 2009

Date:_____ Shooter/Crew:_____ Capture #:_____ Caribou #:_____

R/C Freq.:_____ Serial #:_____ Sex/Age:_____ Group Size:_____

GPS Loc:_____ N _____ W Description:_____

Time	
Start Chase:_____	With Calf/Dam: Yes / No Lactating: Yes / No Est. Age:_____
# Shots:_____	Antler Points: L _____R____ Length: L_____R_____
Time Down:_____	Mandible Length:_____ Neck Circum:_____
Immobilized:_____	Metatarsal Length:_____ Hind Foot:_____
Time Temp:_____	Total Length:_____ Heart Girth:_____
Released:_____	Body Condition Score: 1 2 3 4 5
	Warble Count:_____

Body Weight: _____ **lbs / kg**   **Tare:**_____ **lbs. / kg**   **Collar: On / Off**

Magnet: On / Off / N/A   Body Temp:_____   Pulse/Oximeter:_____

Blood Red:_____ Purple:_____ Green:_____ Tooth (C1):_____ Hair:_____ Fecal:_____

Comments_____

Appendix 3: GPS Collar Specifications

Radiocollars, GPS/ARGOS (Telonics) TGW-4680

    130 sec rep rate, 32 bytes.

    GPS: 3 locations per day (every 8 hours starting at 0000 UTC)

    ARGOS: 6-hour on times every 5 days @ 2000 UTC

    VHF: on 12 hours beginning @1700 UTC (8am - 8 pm AST or 9am - 9pm ADT)

CR-2A collar release mechanism

Collar adjustment range: 16-20", centered on 18"

VHF signal beats:		
	mortality	90 bpm
	Dead battery	20 bpm
	GPS fix	60 bpm
	Missed fix	40 bpm

Cold weather tested

Weight: Approximately 1115 grams

Appendix 4: GPS Data Sharing Agreement

The GPS dataset that is being generated by the Caribou Vital Sign monitoring program has strict use and access constraints. The National Park Service (NPS) stipulates the following conditions with this dataset:

1. This dataset may only be distributed to cooperating wildlife management agencies that are members of the Western Arctic Caribou Herd Working Group (WACHWG).

2. Other entities may obtain and use this dataset only following consultation with the WACHWG and obtaining written permission of the National Park Service.

3. This dataset may not be distributed without the accompanying metadata document.

4. All distribution must originate from the National Park Service in order to ensure that the data is current, of highest quality and well-documented.

5. Users will credit the National Park Service, Alaska Department of Fish and Game, U.S. Fish and Wildlife Service and the WACHWG for the dataset.

6. Users (both cooperating wildlife management agencies and other entities) will notify the principal investigator of the caribou monitoring program of the National Park Service Arctic Network Inventory and Monitoring program of any intent to publish products from this dataset. The NPS strongly encourages cooperative analyses/projects.

Standard Operating Procedure 2: Techniques for Radiotracking of Collared Caribou

Version 1.0 August, 2012, K. Joly

Revision History Log:

Prev. Version #	Revision Date	Author	Changes Made	Reason for Change	New Version #

Scope and Application: This Standard Operating Procedure explains the procedure for radiotracking collared caribou. This SOP also outlines procedures for responding to caribou collar mortality signals. The steps for changing the protocol are outlined in the Revising the Protocol SOP.

Preparation and Equipment Procurement

Procedures:

1. *Procuring equipment for aerial telemetry.* Complete radiotracking systems are available from a number of companies in the United States, Canada and elsewhere. This protocol will recommend the use of particular brands and models of equipment with which the authors are most familiar, with some alternatives mentioned.

   Great technological advances are being made in the development of radio telemetry equipment for wildlife. "Standard" telemetry receivers that received widespread use for twenty or more years are no longer being manufactured, and new models are taking their place. For example, the Telonics TR-2 receiver and TS-1 scanner, manufactured by the same company as the radiocollars recommended in this protocol, are no longer made. They have been replaced by the TR-5 scanning receiver. This procedure will recommend the use of scanning receivers made by Advanced Telemetry Systems, while anticipating the use of receiver/data logger units that may replace the manual recording of data in the near future.

   A highly functional tracking system for small aircraft consists of the following:

Basic system (2011 prices):

Model R8000 telemetry receiver (Advanced Telemetry Systems, Isanti MN)	3200.00
RA-2A directional tracking antenna (pair) (Telonics, Inc, Mesa AZ)	220.00
TAB-3 aircraft antenna brackets for Supercub (pair)	540.00
RW-3-17 coaxial antenna cables, 17 foot (Telonics) (pair)	70.00
RW-2 coaxial cable (to attach switchbox to receiver) (Telonics)	15.00
TAC-2 antenna switchbox (Telonics)	125.00
1/4 " mono phone cable (#42-2381) and splitter (#42-2545) (Radio Shack)	10.00

Alternatives:

Model R4000 telemetry receiver (4 MHz range) (Advanced Telemetry Systems)	2750.00
Model R4500 receiver, GPS, and data logger (Advanced Telemetry Systems)	5800.00
TR-5 scanning receiver (Telonics)	2520.00
R-1000 scanning receiver (Communications Specialists)	695.00
Antenna switchbox (Advanced Telemetry Systems)	95.00

Antennae for handheld, ground tracking:

Model 13863, 3-element folding handheld antenna (Advanced Telemetry Systems)	120.00
RA-14K 2-element flexible "rubber ducky" antenna (Telonics)	212.00

2. *Alternatives.* The basic system listed above will give efficient, durable performance for aerial radiotracking. For an extra fee, Advanced Telemetry Systems will install a signal attenuation switch on the R4000 receiver, which improves its performance for close-range tracking. Superior antenna performance, both in sensitivity to distant signals and directionality for close-range tracking, can be obtained with an alternative antenna mount that changes the orientation of the antennae and moves them away from the metal of the wing strut, by using a wooden dowel that projects forward of the wing. This attachment method has been approved by the Federal Aviation Administration and the AMD Drawings No. AMD-2-8-87, AMD-2-9-87, AMD-2-10-87). All antenna attachments must be performed and logged by a certified aircraft mechanic.

Alternate choices for a telemetry receiver include:
1) the ATS R4000 receiver, which covers a narrower range of frequencies for use on specific projects,
2) the ATS R4500 receiver/GPS/data logger, which records location information internally,
3) the Telonics TR-5 scanning receiver, which can also be configured for data acquisition, and
4) the Communications Specialists R-1000 scanning receiver, a very compact and inexpensive unit that is excellent for handheld tracking and as a backup unit.

In regards to swithboxes, some users prefer the antenna switchbox manufactured by ATS, which has proved to be more durable than the Telonics unit, but is somewhat larger.

For ground-based radiotracking, as when retrieving a collar in mortality mode, the biologists will need a handheld antenna that can be conveniently and safely carried in a vehicle or backpack as needed. The flexible and folding antennae listed above are both good choices.

Aircraft and Pilot procurement and flight preparation

Procedures:

1. *Aircraft and pilot selection.* Aircraft and pilots used for radiotracking by the NPS in Alaska must be procured in accordance with the directives of the AMD. This may include the use of aircraft owned by NPS or AMD, or privately owned aircraft obtained on a contract or rental agreement. Information about aircraft procurement is available from AMD.

    Experience has shown that aerial radiotracking is performed most efficiently when the pilot operates the switchbox, so that the aircraft can be oriented in response to changes in signal strength. This requires a period of training and practice for pilots. Expertise at radiotracking, along with the many challenges of safe flying in the remote and mountainous terrain of Alaska and the harsh weather conditions often encountered, provide strong arguments for careful selection of pilots for this work. Aerial radio telemetry and Alaskan aviation in general are relatively high-risk activities (Sasse 2003, Conway and Moran 2002), and careful selection of aircraft and pilots are necessary to minimize risk.

    The standard aircraft for radio telemetry in Alaska is the Piper PA-18 Supercub. Other aircraft, such as the Christen Husky and the Bellanca Scout, have similar capabilities. The tandem seating allows for full visibility by pilot and passenger when circling in either direction, the ability to fly slowly for effective observations, and the ability to land in a wide variety of locations. These factors have made these aircraft desirable for wildlife work. Occasionally, when long distances must be traveled for telemetry work, or during very short mid-winter days, a faster aircraft such as the Cessna 185 may be favored.

2. *Necessary equipment.* Aircraft used for aerial telemetry and other wildlife work must carry at least one GPS receiver, with an external antenna mounted on the aircraft. Suitable units include the Garmin GPS 150 (panel mounted) and the Garmin GPS 296 (moving map) receivers. Appropriate radio equipment is specified in AMD contracts and FAA regulations, so that aircraft can communicate flight plans, obtain weather information, and notify other aircraft of their presence in certain areas. Radio equipment carried in fixed-wing aircraft is not usually able to communicate on park radio systems. Appropriate equipment can be specified so that this communication can be made, but the very small aircraft used for radio telemetry have limited space for radio equipment. A valuable safety device for communication in remote areas is the satellite telephone, which is becoming increasingly common in Alaska.

    Aerial radiotracking usually involves descending lower than 500 feet above ground level, and therefore qualifies as a "special use" activity under AMD regulations. NPS personnel on radiotracking flights are required to wear PPE, including a Nomex flight suit, all-leather boots and an approved helmet. An exception for winter flying has been arranged between NPS and AMD, that allows warm clothing and footwear that would not otherwise meet PPE standards to be worn on special-use flights, because of their survival value in cold weather.

Programming telemetry receivers

Procedures:

1. *Programming scanning receivers.* Prior to a flight, the radio frequencies of all animals that will be sought are entered into the telemetry receiver's memory bank. Figure 1 shows the control panel of an ATS R8000 telemetry receiver. The R8000 has four memory banks, so that frequencies can be divided into geographic areas to avoid scanning for collars that are not nearby thereby improving the efficiency of the mission. With the receiver turned on and the bypass switch in bypass mode, a memory bank (A,B,C,D) is selected, the last four digits of the desired frequency are dialed in with the four frequency selectors, and the ADD/DELETE switch is pressed momentarily to the ADD position to place the frequency in the memory bank. The procedure is repeated for each desired frequency. Typically, the frequencies that are 1/1000th of a megahertz above and below the desired frequency are also added, in case the frequency has 'drifted' from the frequency of the originally built crystal. This process is known as bracketing.

Newer telemetry receivers like the ATS R4500 can be programmed by direct hookup to a computer database. Another advantageous feature of the R4500 is the availability of animal identity notes on the LCD readout, so that the sex and age of an animal can be seen when the frequency is addressed. This feature is also available on the inexpensive Communications Specialists R-1000 receiver. The receiver needs to be charged according to manufacturer's instructions, before the flight. The operator's manual for the R8000 receiver can be found in the Supplements folder for this monitoring protocol.

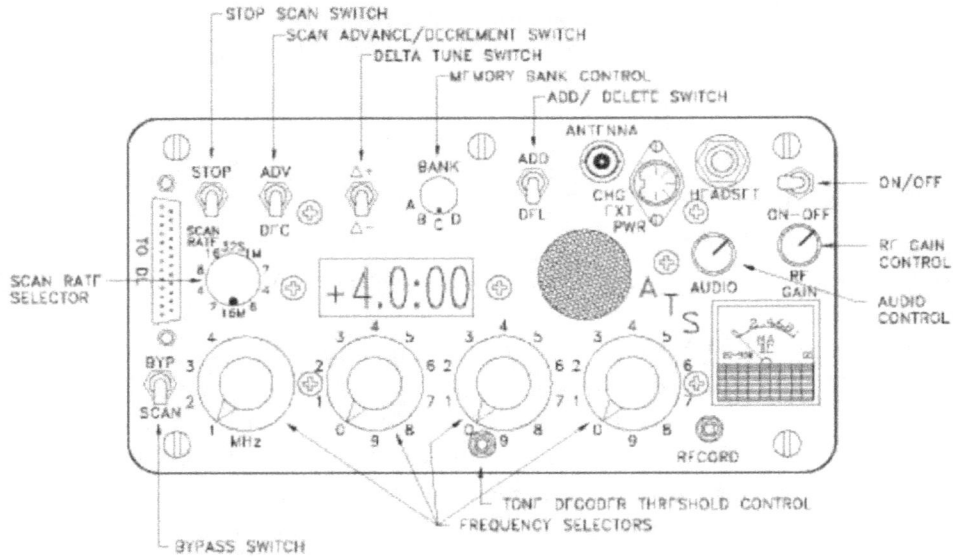

Figure 4. Controls of Advanced Telemetry Systems R-8000 telemetry receiver/scanner.

Aerial Radiotracking

Procedures:

1. System setup. Before beginning an aerial radiotracking flight, the telemetry receiver must be connected to the aircraft's intercom system, and to the antenna system. Coaxial cables from the two wing-mounted antennae connect to a switchbox capable of selecting either the right or left antenna or both at once. A single coaxial cable runs from the switchbox to the antenna connector on the telemetry receiver. The audio output (labeled "headset") on the receiver is connected to the aircraft intercom system with a ¼ inch phone cable, either plugged directly into the intercom (if a dedicated telemetry input is provided) or through a splitter, available at Radio Shack.

2. Homing in on a radiocollar. The aircraft proceeds to the area where the first collared animal is thought to be, with the antenna switchbox in the "both" position, so that signals from both sides of the aircraft can be heard. The RF gain switch on the receiver should be turned all the way up, and the attenuation switch, if present, should be in the off position. The volume knob is adjusted for a comfortable level. When a signal is heard, the scanner is stopped on that frequency, then the switchbox is used to listen to each antenna separately, and the aircraft is turned in the direction of the louder signal. When the aircraft is headed directly toward the source of the signal, the volume from the left and right antenna are equal, or the signal may be lost altogether because neither antenna is pointed toward the signal source. As the radiocollared animal is approached, the RF gain knob is turned progressively lower, and when the signal is quite loud the attenuation switch (if present) is turned on if needed. The lower gain level makes it easier to discriminate between slight differences in signal strength between the two antennae. If the collar is passed, there will be an abrupt decrease in signal strength. The aircraft is maneuvered around the signal while using the switchbox to select between the

34

antennae. When the aircraft is circling the collared animal, the signal from the inside wing is consistently louder, all around the circle. In open country, particularly in winter, the collared animal and other caribou may already have been sighted by this time. If the caribou is concealed by vegetation, it may never be seen, but the accuracy of the tracking system should allow its location to be estimated to within 100 meters or less. Once the pilot and observer have seen the animal or determined its location, the site is waypointed with the aircraft's GPS receiver. Care must be taken to mark the waypoint when the aircraft is directly over the animal location.

3. Data recording. Once a collared caribou has been located, that line on the data sheet is filled out. A key at the bottom of the sheet contains guidelines for recording data. The columns on the data sheet:

TIME: 24 hour time. The example of 13:10 is 10 after 1p.

GRP #: Group number. This is of assistance when multiple collared caribou are found in 1 group.

ACRCY: Accuracy. This quantifies the accuracy of the location. If the collared caribou was actually seen and a good location was determined, then the accuracy would be a "1". A "2" signifies that the collared caribou was within a flight circle but could not be visually located. A designation of "3" is used for collars that were heard but only a general location was determined.

BULL: number of bulls seen

COW: number of cows seen

CALVES: number of calves seen

WITH CALF?: Did the collared cow have a calf with it. "Y" – Yes, "N"- No, "?" – Unknown.

TOTAL: total number of caribou seen in the group with the collared caribou. {*Note: the above numbers include the collared caribou*}

SNOW COVER: Amount of snow cover: B-bare, P-patchy, E-entire, WB-windblown.

SNOW DEPTH: S-shallow (6"), M-moderate (6-12"), D-deep (12+").

TERR: Terrain. STP-steep slope (>45), MOD-moderate slope (20-45), GEN-gentle slope, RID-Ridge, KNO-Knoll, BLU-bluff, F-flat

Veg: Vegetation. DF-deciduous forest, SF-spruce forest, MF-mixed forest, TS-tall shrub, SS-short shrub, T-tundra, TT-tussock tundra, B-Burn, R-Riparian, W-wetland/lake

LATITUDE and LONGITUDE are recorded in degrees, minutes, and decimal minutes or decimal degrees. Latitude and longitude are recorded in the datum WGS84.

{*At present, the coordinates are read from the aircraft GPS and recorded by hand on the data sheet. Waypoints may also be downloaded from the GPS to a computer and pasted into a database. Newer technology like the ATS R4500 receiver may allow location data to be stored in the telemetry receiver itself, eliminating manual transcription and its potential for errors.*}

COMMENTS: description of general location, actions, other animals present, etc.

If associated animals are on adjacent rows of the data sheet, ditto marks can be used to indicate that data is the same. Associated animals should be noted in the comments column.

4. *Continuing the flight.* Once a collared animal has been located, its frequency is deleted from the memory bank for the remainder of the flight. Typically, two or three memory banks on the receiver are used for different geographic areas, with missing or dispersing caribou being programmed into more than one bank. When searching for the next caribou to locate, the attenuation switch (if present) is turned off, the RF gain switch returned to its maximum position, the antenna switchbox is returned to the "both" position, and the aircraft regains altitude. Because VHF telemetry signals are more or less "line of sight", the range at which collars can be heard varies greatly, and increases with increased altitude of the tracking aircraft. Practical range can vary from 60 kilometers or more when an animal is on a mountaintop with nothing between it and the aircraft to less than a kilometer when an animal is in a canyon or behind a mountain.

5. *Timing of radiotracking efforts.* The primary goals of caribou aerial radiotracking are the determination of post-capture status to check on environmental conditions, and to gather a host of environmental information. Calf status (presence/absence), group size and habitat condition and usage data will also be collected. These flights will typically be made in October and April. The April flights may also be used to retrieve collars from mortalities and collect fecal and urine samples for body condition assessments. Individual cooperating agencies may tailor tracking efforts in order to answer specific research or management questions. Examples include the identification of caribou groups for photocensuses or studies of food habits or predation rates. Once the investment has been made to place radiocollars on caribou, it is desirable to get the maximum benefit from the effort for monitoring, research, and management goals.

Response to caribou mortalities

Radiotracking of collared caribou inevitably requires responding to "mortality" signals (collars that are beeping at a different rate because they have been programmed to change transmission rate if motionless for 12 hours). Experience has shown that caribou very seldom remain still long enough for their collars to enter mortality mode while still attached to a living caribou. It can be expected that any collar in mortality mode represents a dead caribou, a collar that has come off of the caribou, or, rarely, a collar with a malfunctioning motion sensor. The fates of individual caribou are a central part of data gathering for population-level monitoring.

In Alaska, investigating caribou mortality signals often requires a helicopter to reach the site. Antenna mounting systems are available for all models of helicopters commonly used for wildlife work, so that the helicopter can track a radio signal. Alternatively, if accurate coordinates were obtained when the mortality signal was first tracked, the helicopter may simply land near those coordinates, allowing the investigators to track in on the collar on the ground. A portable handheld telemetry antenna is needed for this tracking. Folding units, available in rigid (ATS) and flexible (Telonics) models, are convenient to carry and effective. As with aerial telemetry, it is necessary to decrease the gain setting on a receiver as a signal is approached, in order to maintain directionality. At a high gain setting, the signal may seem to be of equal strength at all points of the compass. Decreasing the gain and moving to a different vantage point are the best strategies for overcoming a lack of obvious directionality in a signal. Once the tracker is close to the collar, it may be easiest to disconnect the antenna and simply walk about with the receiver, searching for the loudest signal until the dead caribou or collar are stumbled upon. A signal coming from under snow presents unique difficulties, because a great deal of shoveling may be required to reach the collar. Suspending the receiver, without antenna, over the surface of the snow and moving it about can be very useful in pinpointing where to dig.

Caribou occasionally are able to slip radiocollars off over their heads. This usually happens soon after collaring, particularly when collars are left oversized on a young animal to allow for growth. Caribou are also capable of getting a leg stuck in a loose collar, which can be fatal.

Most collars that are heard in mortality mode will represent actual caribou mortalities. Prompt investigation of mortalities makes it more likely that data regarding the source of mortality will not be lost due to time, environmental conditions, decomposition or scavenging. When a relatively intact carcass is found, necropsy should be performed by experts, such as the veterinarians at the University of Alaska, Institute of Arctic Biology or ADFG. Ideally, a carcass should be refrigerated but not frozen, to preserve histology, but field conditions do not usually allow a choice of storage temperature. If transportation of the carcass is impractical or the remains are too decomposed for necropsy, a field necropsy may be performed. The lower jaw should be collected, if found, so a tooth can be removed to age the individual.

A sample necropsy data form is found in Appendix 2. Although the exact procedures for conducting a field necropsy will vary depending on the conditions encountered in the field, some general guidelines should be followed. By cracking open a femur, humerus or other large leg bone, and examining the color and consistency of the marrow, an idea of the nutritional state of the caribou can be learned. Red, gelatinous or watery bone marrow (or, after drying, a bone with almost nothing in it) indicates a starving caribou. Pink, waxy marrow indicates a better-nourished caribou. The simplest investigation of caribou mortalities should include photographing the site and collection of the jaw bone and a large leg bone. The jaw bone provides an index of the individual's size and age can be estimated from a tooth.

Though while not possible in most circumstances when a significant amount of time has past from the mortality event, it is often useful to try to determine cause of death. A common cause of death for caribou is predation. Blood in the snow, particularly if it is spread about, is indicative of a predation event and can be useful for differentiating between predation and other causes of death. When investigating a site, the investigator should look for hair (from the predator), tracks and scat. With bear kills, the carcass (if any is left) is usually buried in a big mound and bones are crushed and consumed. Obviously, bear predation is rare from November through April. Wolves are much more delicate eaters and they will leave bones, even some of the finer ones intact. These bones may be more scattered than at a bear kill as individuals drag pieces of a carcass away from other pack mates. Wolverine will often bury portions of the carcass in numerous locations, either in snow caves or in boulder field.

Analyses of the GPS coordinates will likely provide an easier means to identify potential caribou mortalities. A query tool within the ARCN locations database ("Am I Dead?") examines the movement or lack thereof of individual caribou and reports back individuals with little to no movement. The individuals are examined in ArcGIS by the caribou project lead to better determine its status. If thought to be a likely mortality, the individual will be a focus of the next radiotracking effort. Also, this information can be relayed to cooperating agencies so they may verify the caribou's status sooner.

Addresses and Contact Information

Caribou necropsy:	Dr. Kimberlee Beckman, DVM	(907) 459-7257
	Alaska Department of Fish and Game	
	1300 College Road	
	Fairbanks, AK 99701-1551	

Dr. John Blake, DVM   (907) 474-5188, (907) 474-5288
Institute of Arctic Biology
Room 311 Irving I Building
P.O. box 757000
University of Alaska, Fairbanks
Fairbanks, AK 99775-7000
http://www.uaf.edu/iacuc/vet/

Telemetry Equipment: Telonics, Inc.   (602) 892-4444
932 E. Impala Ave.
Mesa, AZ 85204-6699
www.telonics.com

Advanced Telemetry Systems   (763) 444-9267
470 First Avenue North
Box 398
Isanti, MN 55040
www.atstrack.com

Communications Specialists Inc.   (800) 854-0547
426 West Taft Ave.
Orange, California 92865-4224
http://www.com-spec.com/r1000/r1000.htm

Flight suits, PPE   Gibson & Barnes   (800) 440-5904
1675 Pioneer Way
El Cajon, CA 92020
www.flightsuits.com

Aircraft Procurement   USDI Aviation Management Directorate   (907) 271-3700
& Aircraft Safety Training   4405 Lear Court
Anchorage, AK 99502-1032
http://amd.nbc.gov

Map software for   ESRI   (800) 447-9778
data verification   380 New York Street
Redlands, CA 92373-8100

References

Advanced Telemetry Systems. 2004. Receiver models R2000/R2100/R4000. Receiver manual R01-02-A. Advanced Telemetry Systems, Isanti MN.

Conway, G., and K. Moran. 2002. Factors associated with pilot fatalities in work-related aircraft crashes - Alaska, 1990-1999. Morbidity and Mortality Weekly Report 51(16): 347-349.

Gilmer, D. S., L. M. Cowardin, R. L. Duval, L. M. Mechlin, C. W. Schaiffer, and V. B. Kuechle. 1981. Procedures for the use of aircraft in wildlife biotelemetry studies. USFWS Resource Publication 140. 19 pp.

Mech, L. D. 1983. Handbook of Animal Radiotracking. University of Minnesota Press.

Sasse, D. B. 2003. Job-related mortality of wildlife workers in the United States, 1937-2000. Wildlife Society Bulletin 31(4): 1015-1020.

Seddon, P. J., and R. F. Maloney. Tracking wildlife radio-tag signals by light fixed-wing aircraft. Department of Conservation Technical Series No. 30, New Zealand Department of Conservation, Wellington, New Zealand. 23pp.

Appendix 1: Caribou Radiotracking Data Form

	A	B	C	D	E	F	G	H	I	J	K	L	M	N	O	P	Q	R
1	WAH Caribou			Radiotracking Data		Page 1 of ____											Revised	7/27/2009
2																	Time Up:	_____
3	Date:		Plane:			Pilot:							Observer:				Time Down:	_____
4	Weather:																Total Flight Time:	
5	ID	Freq	Old Cmmnt	Time	Grp #	Acrcy	Bull	Cow	Calves	with calf?	Total	Snow Cover	Snow Depth	Terr	Veg	Latitude	Longitude	Comment (Cratering, Location, Kills, etc)
6	09-01	148.740	Kobuk	13:10	1	1	0	1	1	Y	2	WB	B	KNO	T	64.79523	-159.97234	Nulato Hills, feeding
7																		
8																		
9																		
10																		
11																		
12																		
13																		
14																		
15																		
16																		
17																		
18																		
19																		
20																		
21																		
22																		
23																		
24																		
25																		
26																		
27																		
28																		
29																		
30																		
31																		
32																		
33	Terrain-STP-steep slope (>45), MOD-moderate slope (20-45), GEN-gentle slope, RID-Ridge,									Snow cover: B-bare, P-patchy, E-entire, WB-windblown								
34	KNO-Knoll, BLU-bluff, F-flat									Snow depth: S-shallow (6"), M-moderate (6-12"), D-deep (12+")								
35	Veg: DF-deciduous forest, SF-spruce forest, MF-mixed forest, TS-tall shrub, SS-short shrub, T-tundra, TT-									Accuracy: 1=visual, 2= no visual, signal from within a circle, 3=general								
36	tussock tundra, B-Burn, R-Riparian, W-wetland/lake									area								

Appendix 2: Sample Caribou Necropsy Data Form

WAH CARIBOU NECROPSY RECORD   Necropsy No:_____
                                         Caribou No:_____
                                    Frequency:_____

Date died:_____Date examined:_____
Last heard alive:_____ First heard in mort:_____
Lat:_____deg._____._____min.N Long:_____deg._____._____min.W

_____

Age_____ Sex_____ Body length_____ Chest girth _____

Specimens examined:

    General condition_____
    Subcutaneous fat_____
    Omental and kidney fat_____
    Xiphoid fat: _____ grams
    Femur marrow: appearance_____ % fat_____
    Stomach contents_____
    Parasites_____
    Tooth wear_____

Specimens collected:

    Entire Carcass _____
    Skull_____Mandible_____Long bone_____
    Reproductive tract: Collected_____
        Analysis_____
    Tissues: Heart_____Liver_____Kidney_____Muscle_____
    Femur/femur marrow:_____ Radiocollar: _____
    Blood: whole_____
        serum_____
    Urine_____
    Other_____

Comments (cause of death?):_____
_____
_____
_____
_____

Carcass Retrieved by: _____
Hunter or trapper: _____ Reward paid?_____
Necropsy by: _____

Standard Operating Procedure 3: Handling GPS/ARGOS Location Data

Version 1.0 August, 2012, K. Joly

Revision History Log:

Prev. Version #	Revision Date	Author	Changes Made	Reason for Change	New Version #

Acquiring location data from radiocollars

Western Arctic Herd (WAH) caribou monitoring projects led by the ADFG have used two types of radiocollars on caribou. The first type, first used in the 1970s, is a VHF transmitter mounted on a flexible collar, which can be tracked from an aircraft so that the caribou can be located and observed. The second type, first used in the 1980s, is the VHF/ARGOS collar, which, in addition to the conventional VHF transmitter, contains systems that determine the collar's location using the ARGOS satellites, stores location data inside the collar, and periodically uploads location information through the ARGOS satellite system. The ARCN protocol updates caribou monitoring by deploying a third type, the Telonics GPS/ARGOS collar. These new collars contain systems that determine the collar's location using the GPS and then transmit this data using the ARGOS satellite system.

The GPS consists of approximately 30 medium-Earth orbit satellites (orbiting at an elevation of 20,200 km) that transmit precisely timed radio signals. GPS receivers use the signals from four or more satellites to calculate their location. GPS/ARGOS animal collars determine their location at some pre-programmed interval and time (in the case of the caribou collars used in ARCN monitoring, the location is determined 3 times daily). The collars have sufficient data storage capability to store all locations determined during the lifespan of the collar, typically 2.5 to 3 years. In addition, the location data can be accessed in a timelier manner by using a radio signal to upload the data. Telonics GPS/ARGOS collars are identified by a unique ARGOS numerical code, and upload the data to the ARGOS satellite system, a set of polar-orbiting satellites located 850 km above the earth. Transmitters are programmed to send signals to satellites at periodic intervals. The GPS/ARGOS collars currently in use are programmed to upload caribou location data every 4 days. ARGOS satellites receive and store the data, and relay the data to a system of ground antennae. ARGOS processing centers (in the U.S., operated by CLS America in Largo, MD) collect and process incoming data and distribute them to users. Caribou location data is received from CLS America via email in batches that contain all of the data that was received in a given day.

GPS/ARGOS caribou collars provide over 1000 locations per year for collared animals, greatly increasing the sample size of locations that can be used to calculate caribou seasonal ranges and movement rates. Caribou must still be located from aircraft, using VHF collars or the VHF beacons on GPS/ARGOS collars, in order to observe the group sizes, count calves, locate cratering in snow, and other data that can only be obtained from direct visual observation. Combining conventional telemetry with GPS/ARGOS location data provides the optimal technology for monitoring the status and movements of caribou efficiently while minimizing cost and the intrusion of aircraft overflights over park areas.

Procedures

1. System setup.

An administrative page on the NPS/UAF website (http://nuna.uaf.edu:8080/argos/submit_argos_data.php) is used to maintain the list of active ARGOS identification codes, a unique animal ID, species, park, location (e.g., physical feature such as a river name), capture date, collar ID, and model of Telonics GPS/ARGOS collar. This portion of the webpage is password protected. Click the "ADD" button on the main administrative page. On the next page, the user should type in the decimal ARGOS ID for the new collars in the gray section on the bottom left. The collar model (Gen 3 or Gen 4) must be specified from the drop down menu because different data encryption and decoding algorithms are used on the older and newer model collars. Then click the "ADD" button. The new collar ID(s) will now be available on the drop down menu under "Collar ID". Enter in the species, park, capture date, animal ID (user assigned), location (physical feature such as a lake that can be used as an identifier) and collar ID. By including the capture date in the administrative database, a complete history of collar use and re-use is maintained, so that data from any time period can be processed. Click "Add Record" to add the new collar to the system. It should show up on the main administrative page.

The "TPF" file, provided by the collar manufacturer, must be uploaded to the system within the administrative page. This file houses the technical specification of the collars. Each collar must reference its appropriate "TPF" file. Click the "TPF" button on top right of the main page to upload this file. Type in the file name on the next page or use the "Browse..." button to navigate to it and then click the "Upload" button. The TPF file will be listed but still needs to be scanned. Click the radio button by it to select it and then click "Scan". The collar IDs associated with the TPF file should now be listed.

2. Raw data processing.

Location data from Telonics GPS/ARGOS collars (currently the Telonics Gen 4 collar system) is encrypted to conserve bandwidth, and must be decoded using Telonics' proprietary Telonics Data Converter[©] (TDC) software. NPS contracted Dr. Edward DeBevec, of the University of Alaska Fairbanks, to produce a web-based platform incorporating TDC and other functions, so that ARGOS data can easily be decoded, checked for anomalous or redundant values, tagged with caribou numbers, and other identifying information, and stored in an Excel spreadsheet. Using this website and a GIS program such as ArcGIS, caribou locations can be placed on a map and examined within minutes of the reception of the email containing the data.

ARGOS location data is received as text in an email message. Multiple ARGOS emails received from CLS America can be strung together for processing by marking them in Lotus Notes and forwarding them to create a single message. Text data is then exported using the File/Export function in Lotus Notes, designating a name and location for the resulting text message, changing the Word Wrap Within Documents setting (in a popup box) to "Wrap Words at 100 Characters Per Line," and exporting the file. The text save should be saved in the following directory: O:\Monitoring\Vital Signs\Caribou\Data\1-Raw data files\GPS.

On the NPS/UAF ARGOS website (http://nuna.uaf.edu:8080/argos/submit_argos_data.php), the input file can be specified, and dropdown boxes used to select the park unit of interest and to choose between one location per day (appropriate for wolf collars currently deployed by the Central Alaska Network) and multiple locations per day (for collars currently deployed by Arctic Network on caribou). Latitude and longitude fields may need to be adjusted to allow for the large geographical range of the WAH. When the "Submit" button is pushed, the location data appears onscreen. To produce an Excel file, data fields can be selected in the box at the bottom of the page and the "Download" button pressed. The Excel file should be saved in the following directory: O:\Monitoring\Vital Signs\Caribou\Data\2-ConvertedRawData\GPS. Use the "ARCN Data Importer" tool to bring non-redundant data into the master location database. The database locations can be displayed as an event layer in ArcGIS, which can be converted into an ArcGIS shapefile by "right clicking" on the event layer and using the "Data-Export Data" function.

References

CLS America ARGOS data services: http://www.clsamerica.com/

NPS/UAF ARGOS processing site: http://nuna.uaf.edu:8080/argos/submit_argos_data.php

Telonics GPS/ARGOS wildlife systems: http://telonics.com/products/gps4/

Standard Operating Procedure 4: Data Analysis Including Estimating Caribou Seasonal Ranges, Migration Patterns and Survivorship from GPS Data

Version 1.0 August, 2012, K. Joly

Revision History Log:

Prev. Version #	Revision Date	Author	Changes Made	Reason for Change	New Version #

Procedures

1. *Data sorting and validation.* Global Positioning System (GPS) data are made up of locations of individual collared caribou. Caribou migration patterns and survivorship are estimated based on the data of individual caribou. However, seasonal range use will be determined by combining the data of all individual caribou within comparable age/sex classes (if captures are conducted exclusively at Onion Portage, then there will be just a single age/sex class, adult females). Errors in the recording of caribou locations should have been detected, flagged and eliminated in the data verification process described in the Handling GPS/ARGOS Location Data SOP. Additionally, caribou locations are imported into an appropriate map program and locations are visually inspected for gross errors.

2. *Determining caribou distribution from GPS data.* When data have been validated, a home range program (e.g., Rodgers et al. 2007) is used to generate 50% and 95% utilization distribution polygons using fixed kernel analyses (Seaman and Powell 1996) for year round distribution as well as for different, distinct and important biological periods. These periods are defined by biological events that might logically affect caribou distribution; calving, insect relief, summer, and winter. These seasons are defined using predefined dates identified in the literature (Russell et al. 1993, Dau 2007, Person et al. 2007) and using the movement rates of the caribou themselves. The predefined dates are: calving May 25 – June 14; insect relief June 15-July 14; summer July 15- August 31; winter December 15 – April 14. Changes in the distribution, movement rates, and variance in movement rates will be utilized to allow for the caribou themselves to define different seasons (as a second method of defining seasons). Points of inflection will be used to differentiate these changes in seasons.

3. *Determining migration patterns.* Migration patterns will be analyzed on an individual basis, though summary results may average findings for all collared caribou on an annual basis. The location of movement routes and as well the timing of migration will be monitored. For each caribou the following important dates will be calculated; crossing of Noatak, Selawik and

Kobuk rivers and closest distance to the villages of Noatak, Selawik, and Shungnak. Closest distance to each of these villages will also be recorded. Other parameters collected will be total distance traveled August 15-October 14 and annually (September 1-August 31), identification of non- or semi- migratory individuals, and usage/non-usage of key locations (e.g., Howard Pass).

4. *Survivorship.* The survival of our sample of collared caribou provides valuable life history data on this species in areas where they face relatively high human harvest.

5. *Other caribou population parameters.* In addition to the distribution of monitored caribou, other data may be collected. The causes of death for collared caribou, obtained by examining and retrieving caribou carcasses, are valuable for understanding population dynamics. Trends in the morphology, disease profile, and genetic makeup of caribou, from data gathered in conjunction with capture and population monitoring, may prove to be important to herd management.

6. *Analysis of caribou parameters changes over time.* Caribou populations change dramatically over time. Changes in herd size can lead to changes in distribution, range use and survivorship. These changes are often cyclical. These variations make it difficult to identify changes that may have biological significance, or that could serve as warnings of ecosystem degradation. Analysis of archived wildlife population data maintained by the Alaska Department of Fish and Game may allow models to be built, allowing some predictions of caribou numbers and movement patterns. Overlaying genetic and radiotelemetry data may assist in clarifying timing of breeding events, migration, dispersal patterns and levels of relatedness within and among herds. It will remain a challenge to interpret changes in caribou numbers and distribution, and to identify truly unusual events.

Reporting of Caribou Monitoring Data

Procedures

1. *General features of monitoring reports.* Reports generated by the caribou monitoring effort, and the vital signs monitoring program in general, will be promptly produced, appropriate to their target audience, widely available, and visually accessible. Concise summaries will be a part of each report produced. Reports will conform to guidelines set by the Arctic Monitoring Network and the Alaska Region Inventory and Monitoring Plan. Graphical methods, maps, and other visual aids will be used to make results readily understood.

2. *Annual administrative report and workplan.* These reports are designed to be incorporated into annual Reports to Congress on the nationwide Vital Signs Monitoring Program. The annual administrative report will be produced in the fall of each year. The report will account for the expenditure of funds and FTEs, and describe the objectives, tasks, accomplishments, and products of the monitoring effort during the previous fiscal year. The annual work plan will be completed in the winter of each year and will project the anticipated budget, FTEs and objectives and tasks for the current fiscal year. These reports are designed to improve communication within each park, the Arctic Network, the Alaska Region, and the National Monitoring Program. Their intended audience includes park superintendents, network staff,

regional coordinators, and Service-wide program managers. These reports will be written by the park biologists implementing the caribou monitoring protocol, and reviewed and approved by ARCN, Regional Office and Service-wide Program managers.

3. *Annual report.* A Natural Resource Data Series report will be prepared for publication each October, reporting on caribou monitoring activities during the previous year (September 1 - August 31). The annual report will provide a summary of all caribou monitoring activities and data for the year, and describe the current condition of the caribou population in the areas monitored. Any changes in monitoring protocols will be documented. The intended audience for the annual report includes park resource managers, network staff, and external scientists. The report will be written by the park biologists implementing the caribou monitoring protocol, and peer-reviewed within the Arctic Monitoring Network.

4. *Other reporting.* In addition to the two scheduled annual reports, results of the caribou monitoring effort will be presented at ARCN Vital Signs Monitoring meetings and conference, and at other symposia, conferences, and workshops. Caribou monitoring data will be provided to park interpretive staff for written and oral presentation to visitors. Significant findings will be reported in scientific journals and popular publications.

References

Breck, S. W. and D. E. Biggins. 1997. Detecting and eliminating errors in radio-telemetry data sets: a comparison of screened and unscreened data. U.S. Geological Survey Forum on Wildlife Telemetry: Innovations, Evaluations, and Research Needs; 21-23 September 1997, Snowmass Village, Colorado. Program and Abstracts. U.S. Geological Survey and The Wildlife Society. Jamestown, ND: Northern Prairie Wildlife Research Center. http://www.npwrc.usgs.gov/resource/tools/telemtry/telemtry.htm

Dau, J. 2007. Units 21D, 22A, 22B, 22C, 22D, 22E, 23, 24 and 26A caribou management report. Pages 174-231 *in* P. Harper, editor. Caribou management report of survey and inventory activities 1 July 2004-30 June 2006. Alaska Department of Fish and Game. Project 3.0. Juneau, AK.

Rodgers, A.R., A.P. Carr, H.L. Beyer, L. Smith, and J.G. Kie. 2007. HRT: Home Range Tools for ArcGIS. Ontario Ministry of Natural Resources, Centre for Northern Forest Ecosystem Research, Thunder Bay, Ontario, Canada.

Seaman, D.E. and R.A. Powell. 1996. An evaluation of the accuracy of kernel density estimators for home range analysis. Ecology 77:2075-2085.

White, G. C. and R. A. Garrott. 1990. Analysis of Wildlife Radio-Tracking Data. Academic Press, Inc., San Diego.

Standard Operating Prodedure 5: Generating GPS Data Quality Report

Version 1.0 August, 2012, S.D. Miller

Revision History Log:

Prev. Version #	Revision Date	Author	Changes Made	Reason for Change	New Version #

Scope and Application

GPS collars generate copious amounts of data that must be entered into the caribou monitoring database in batches on a weekly basis. The quality of this data must be assessed immediately after entry and this is done through the use of a database script. The script applies a series of quality assessment queries and provides the results in a report that can guide further action.

Procedures

1. Open SQL Server Management Studio 2008.

2. Open O:\Monitoring\Vital Signs\Caribou\Data\Database\SQL Server Quality Control Scripts and Reports\ARCN_CaribouDataQualityReport.sql

3. Right click on the script text and select 'Results to grid'

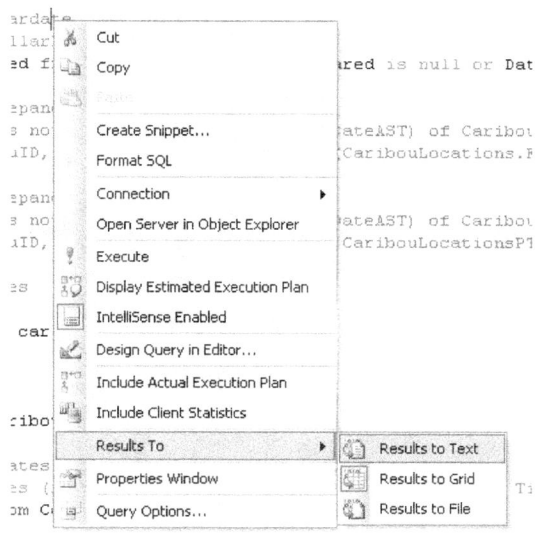

4. Execute the script. The results will appear below the script text window

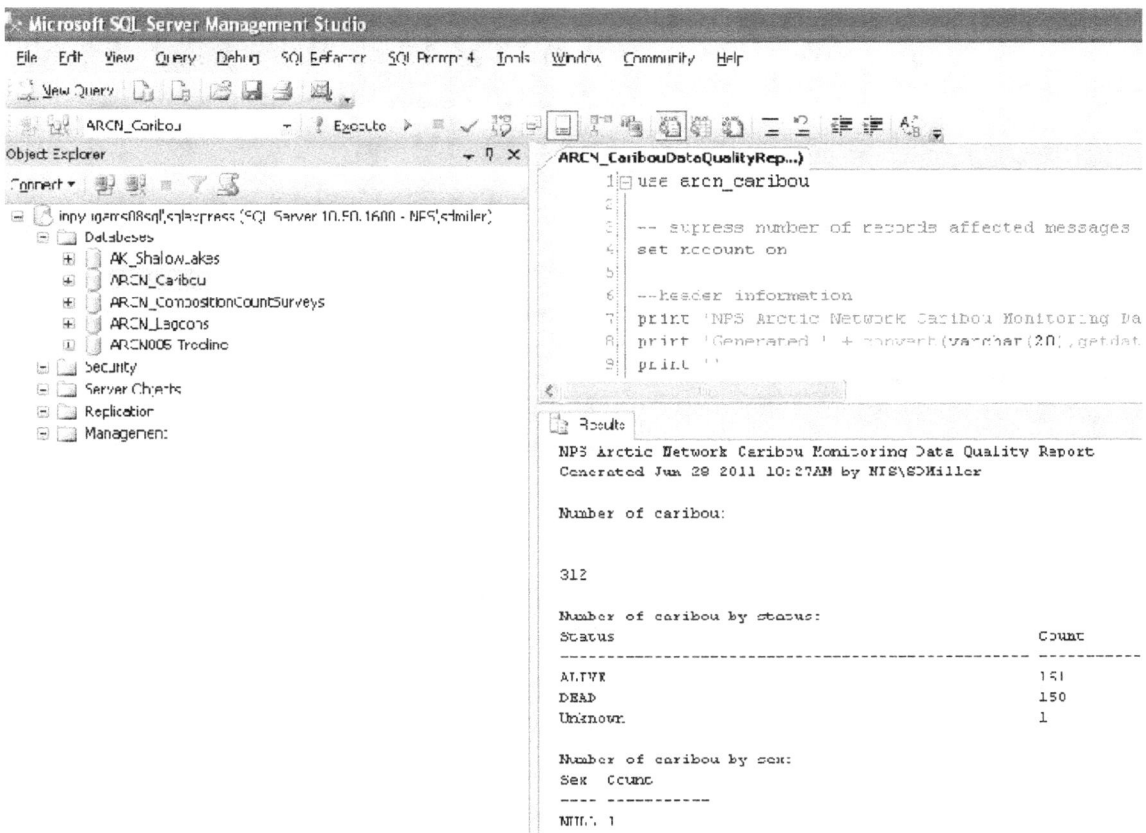

5. Copy and paste the results to O:\Monitoring\Vital Signs\Caribou\Data\Database\SQL Server Quality Control Scripts and Reports following the existing naming structure (yyyy-mm-dd ARCN_CaribouDataQualityReport.txt).

6. Examine the report and alert the PI to any problems.

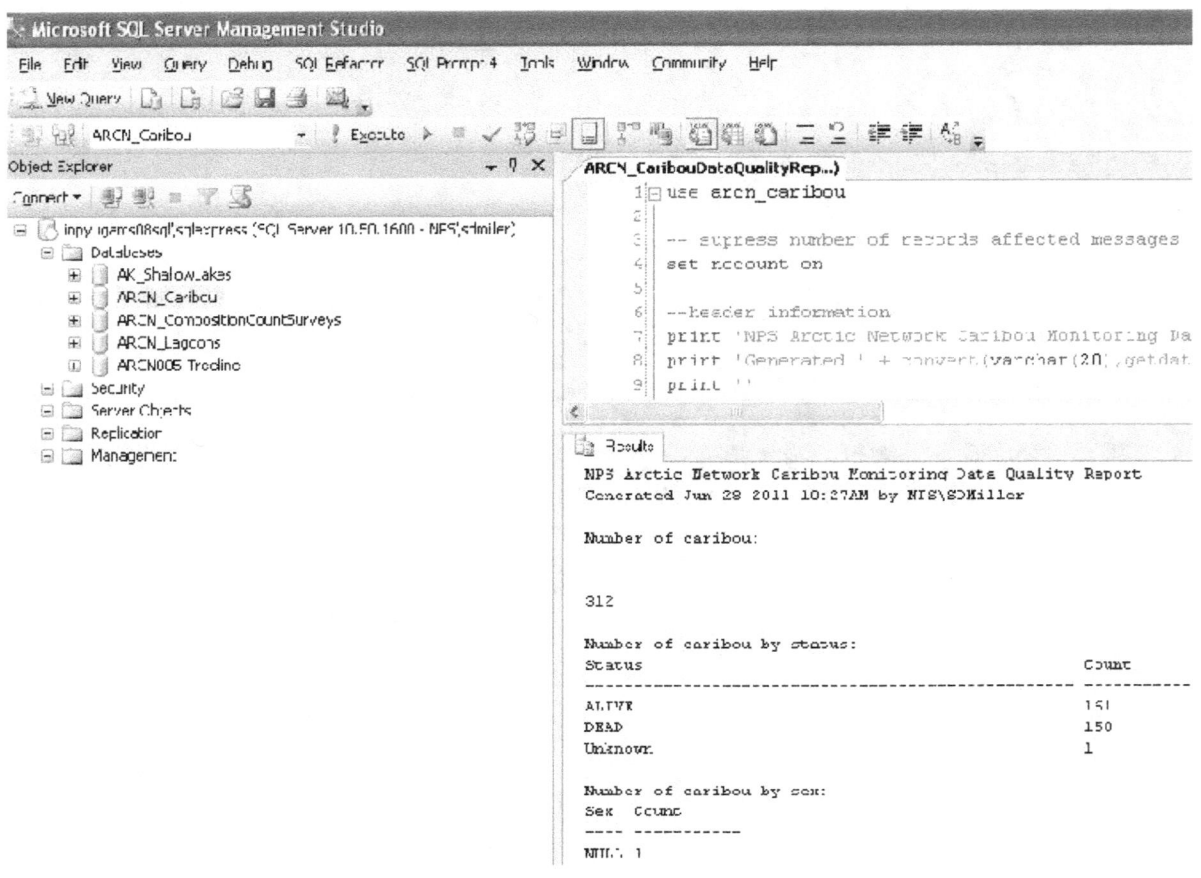

Standard Operating Procedure 6: Western Arctic Herd Working Group

Version 1.0 August, 2012, K. Joly

Revision History Log:

Prev. Version #	Revision Date	Author	Changes Made	Reason for Change	New Version #

Background

The Western Arctic Caribou Herd (WACH) is cooperatively managed by several land management agencies, including the NPS, FWS, BLM and ADFG. The Western Arctic Caribou Herd Working Group (WACHWG) is an advisory group that provides guidance to these agencies. The WACHWG is comprised of stakeholders including representatives of local villages, sport hunters, transporters, guides, reindeer herders, and conservationists. Agency personnel support the group but do not having voting authority. The WAHWG developed a management plan with the purpose to "work together to ensure the long-term conservation of the Western Arctic Caribou Herd and the ecosystem on which it depends, to maintain traditional and other uses for the benefit of all people now and in the future".

Technical Committee

The Technical Committee, comprised of agency personnel and some Working Group members, advises the Working Group, but does not having voting authority. The biologist acting as Lead for the Arctic Network Caribou Monitoring program will be designated as the NPS' representative on the Technical Committee. The Technical Committee member shall prepare for, attend, and contribute to Technical Committee meetings. Meetings are typically held once or twice a year.

Reporting of Caribou Monitoring Data to Working Group

The Working Group is comprised of representatives of Native villages, hunting organizations, and other groups that are interested in the well-being of the WAH. These representatives have voting rights, though the group strives to work in consensus fashion. The NPS Technical Committee will be responsible for reporting caribou monitoring results and NPS contributions to the cooperative program to the WAHWG.

References

Western Arctic Caribou Herd Working Group. 2003. Western Arctic Caribou Herd Cooperative Management Plan. 33 pp.

Standard Operating Procedure 7: Revising the Protocol

Version 1.0 August, 2012, S.D. Miller

Revision History Log:

Prev. Version #	Revision Date	Author	Changes Made	Reason for Change	New Version #

This Standard Operating Procedure explains how to make changes to the Caribou Monitoring Protocol Narrative for the Arctic Monitoring Network, and accompanying SOPs, and tracking these changes. Observers asked to edit the Protocol Narrative or any one of the SOPs need to follow this outlined procedure in order to eliminate confusion in how data is collected and analyzed. All observers should be familiar with this SOP in order to identify and use the most current methodologies.

Procedures

1. The Caribou Monitoring Protocol Narrative for the Arctic Monitoring Network (ARCN) and accompanying SOPs have attempted to incorporate the most sound methodologies for collecting and analyzing caribou distribution, condition and population data. However, all protocols, regardless of how sound, require editing as new and different information becomes available. Required edits should be made in a timely manner and appropriate reviews undertaken.

2. All edits require review for clarity and technical soundness. Small changes or additions to existing methods will be reviewed in-house by ARCN staff. However, if a complete change in methods is sought, than an outside review is required. Regional and National staff of the NPS with familiarity in large mammal research and data analysis will be utilized as reviewers. Also, experts in caribou research and statistical methodologies outside of the NPS will be utilized in the review process.

3. Document edits and protocol versioning in the Revision History Log that accompanies the Protocol Narrative and each SOP. Log changes in the Protocol Narrative or SOP being edited only. Version numbers increase incrementally by hundredths (e.g. version 1.01, version 1.02, ...etc) for minor changes. Major revisions should be designated with the next whole number (e.g., version 2.0, 3.0, 4.0 ...). Record the previous version number, the date

of revision, and the author of the revision. Identify paragraphs and pages where changes are made, and the reason for making the changes along with the new version number.

4. Inform the Data Manager about changes to the Protocol Narrative or SOP so the new version number can be incorporated in the Metadata of the project database. The database may have to be edited by the Data Manager to accompany changes in the Protocol Narrative and SOPs. Post new versions on the inter-net and forward copies to all individuals with a previous version of the affected Protocol Narrative or SOP.

Standard Operating Procedure 8: GPS Data Entry

Version 1.0 August, 2012, S.D. Miller

Revision History Log:

Prev. Version #	Revision Date	Author	Changes Made	Reason for Change	New Version #

GPS location data entry

GPS collar location data is entered into the database using the Arctic Network Caribou GPS Location Data Importer tool. This tool is available for download on the Arctic Network website and the following url:
http://science.nature.nps.gov/im/units/arcn/data_management/software.cfm. The website uses Microsoft ClickOnce framework through Internet Explorer. The software can be downloaded and installed using other browsers but will require more steps to accomplish.

Procedures

1. Open the Arctic Network Caribou GPS Location Data Importer tool
2. Select a workbook to import
3. Select the worksheet containing the location data (the tool usually does this for you).
4. Click '3. Import locations'
5. The tool fills with data (Figure).
6. Click '4. Insert the records into the database'
7. The tool will then attempt to insert the records into the database

Notes

- The tool concatenates data from and eliminates duplicate records in the workbook and updates any existing records in the SQL Server database having null values.

- There may be numerous error messages shown in the output window at the bottom. These errors are mostly messages from the SQL Server informing you that the record being inserted already exists. This is a good thing; quite often there is overlap of GPS fixes among workbooks. The first few dozen records have often already been inserted from the last workbook entered (though often without temperature data) and will cause insertion errors. Ignore them. Also note that if a record exists already with a null temperature, the tool issues an update query to update the existing record with the temperature.

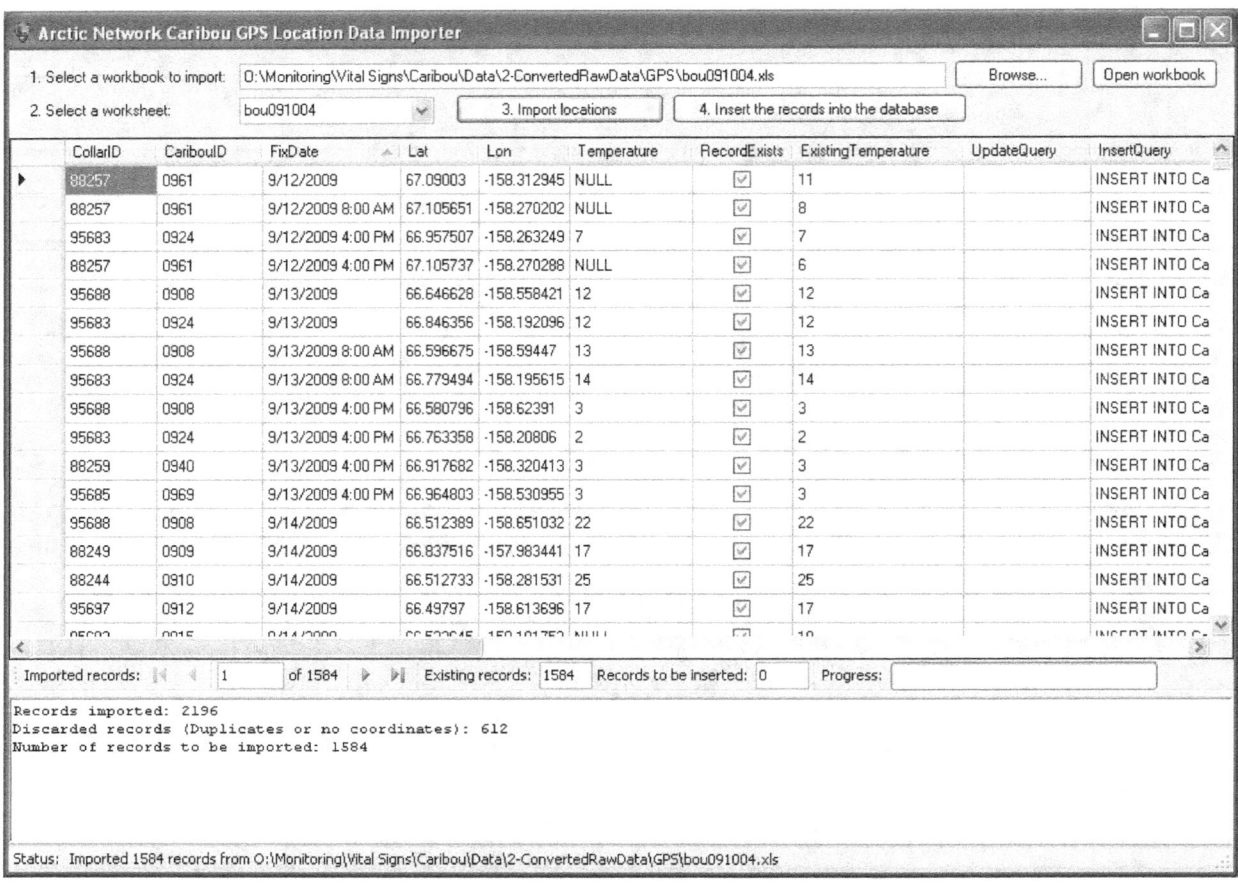

Figure 5. Arctic Network Caribou GPS Data Importer tool.

56

Standard Operating Procedure 9: Data Certification

Version 1.0 August, 2012, S.D. Miller

Revision History Log:

Prev. Version #	Revision Date	Author	Changes Made	Reason for Change	New Version #

The final step in the data lifecycle is certification. Only data that has passed all quality control checks should be certified for publication. This SOP describes the certification process.

Procedures

1. Open the caribou monitoring database
2. Click 'Certify data' on the main menu
3. Read the instructions and click 'Certify current database snapshot'
4. The tool will certify any uncertified records in the database. The output log will relay any problems encountered during certification.

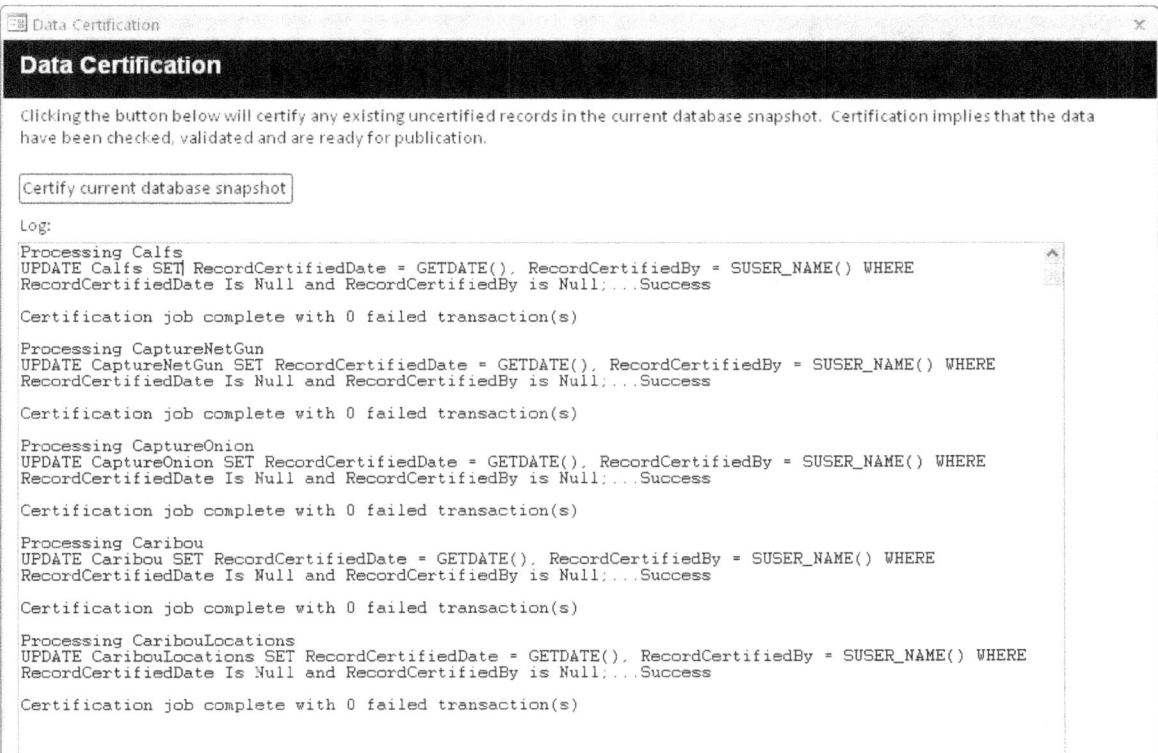

Standard Operating Procedure 10: Exporting Data for Publication

Version 1.0 August, 2012, S.D. Miller

Revision History Log:

Prev. Version #	Revision Date	Author	Changes Made	Reason for Change	New Version #

Sensitivity Statement

IMPORTANT: The caribou monitoring data is considered sensitive and should not be published beyond the Western Arctic Caribou Herd Working Group (WACHWG). Distribution of the data must be accompanied by FGDC metadata and adhere to the conditional use statement in Appendix 5. **The principal investigator and the network coordinator are the only people authorized to distribute caribou monitoring data.**

Scope and Application

Caribou GPS data should be published annually to the WACHWG. The database view 'vwGPSDataPublication' was designed to efficiently view and export certified data. Only certified records will show in the view. If you don't see the records you were expecting make sure the data has been certified. The object of this SOP to get the data from the caribou monitoring database's vwGPSDataPublication view into an ESRI Shapefile.

Materials, Resources and Prerequisites

1. Read privileges on the ARCN_Caribou database
2. Read/Write privileges on the ARCN network drive
3. Microsoft Access 2007
4. ESRI ArcGIS
5. At least one certified row in both the Caribou and CaribouLocations database tables

Exporting GPS data to ArcGIS

Procedures:
1. Start ArcMap
2. Click 'Add data'

3. Connect to the ARCN_Caribou database (if you have not already set up a database connection in ArcMap or ArcCatalog follow the directions in 'Creating an ArcGIS Database Connection' below and then come back to this step.

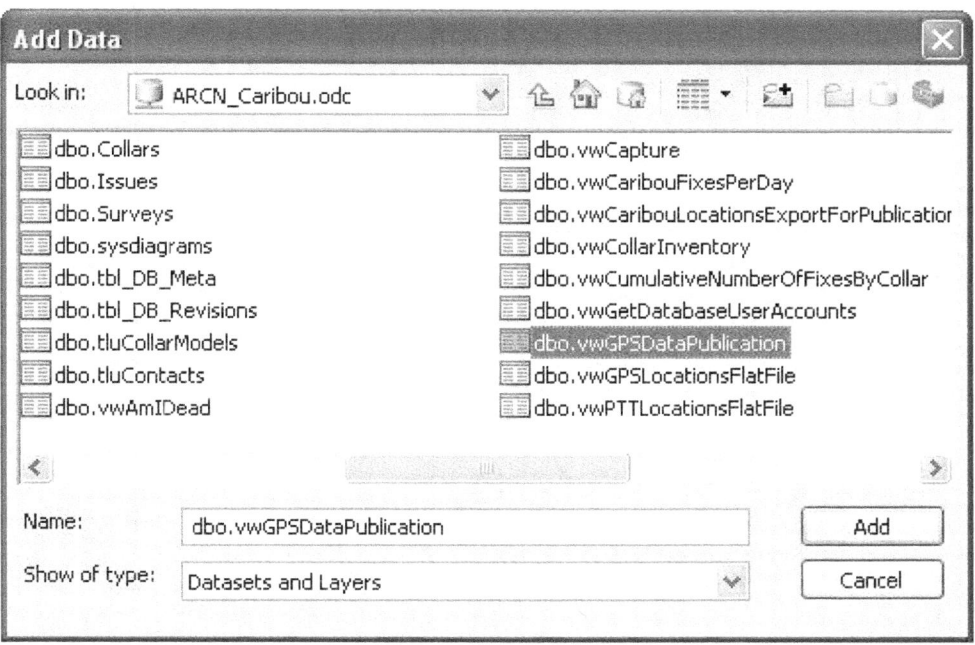

4. Convert the data to an events layer by clicking 'Display XY Data…'.
5. The Display XY Data dialog box comes up.

6. Ensure the form looks like the example here and ensure that the coordinate system is correctly set to WGS84 Geographic

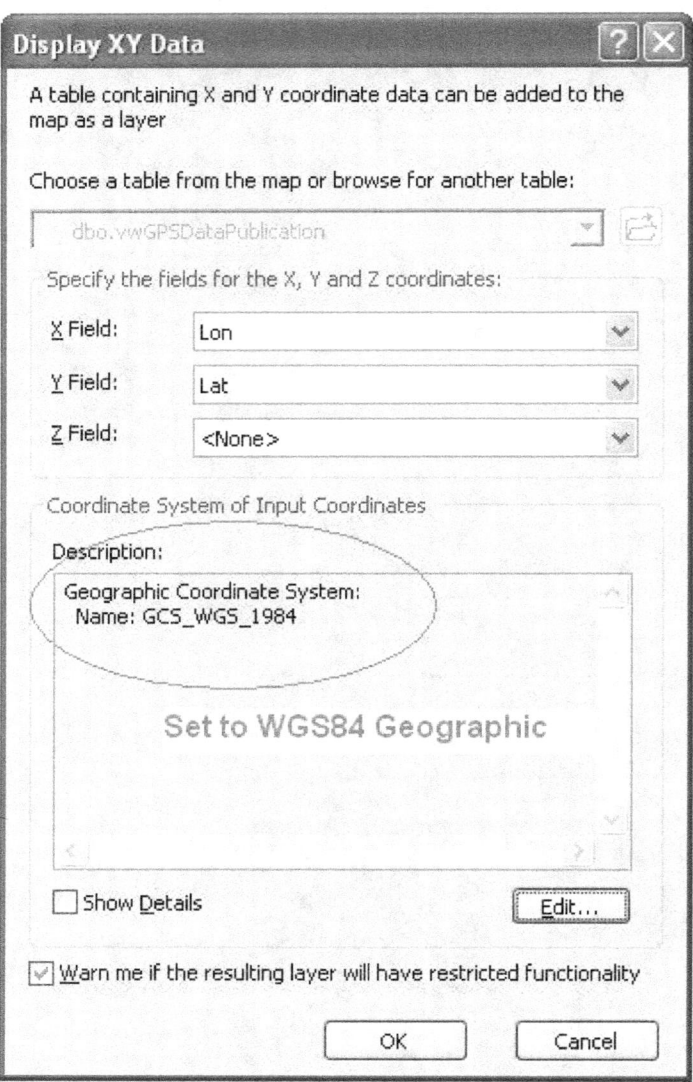

7. A warning will appear informing you that the events layer you are creating will be read-only. Click OK.

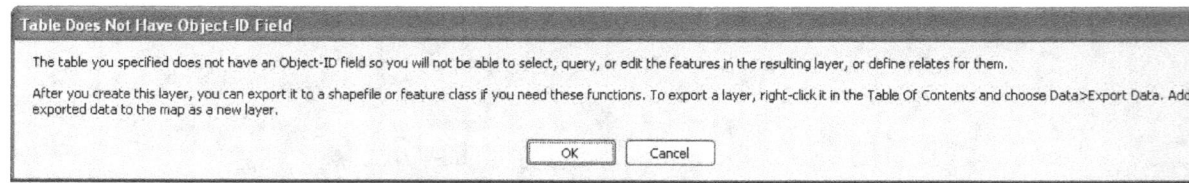

8. Right-click the events layer, click 'Data' and then 'Export Data...'

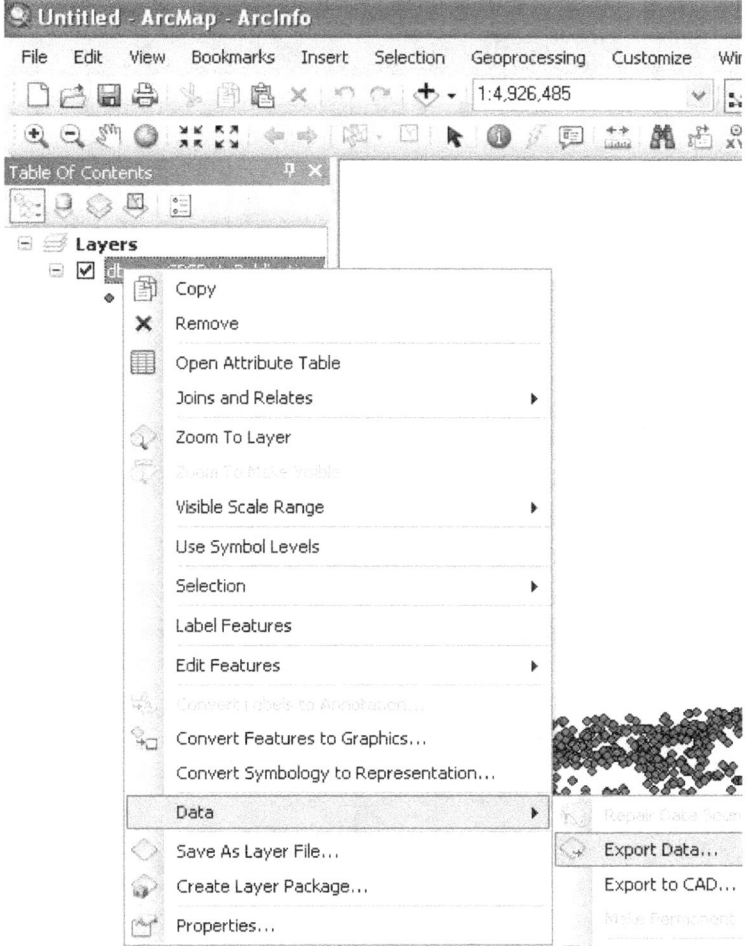

9. Export the data in shapefile format to O:\Monitoring\Vital Signs\Caribou\Data\Data Publication\ARCN_CaribouGPSDate_yyyy-mm-dd.shp where yyyy-mm-dd format corresponds to the current date.

The next step before distributing the data is to create FGDC metadata for the shapefile. See SOP 11 for details.

Creating an ArcGIS Database Connection

The following workflow shows how to set up an ArcGIS database connection to the ARCN_Caribou SQL Server database. This process is the quickest way to import GPS data to ArcMap.

1. In ArcCatalog or using the 'Add Data' tool in ArcMap navigate to the 'Database Connections' node and click 'Add'

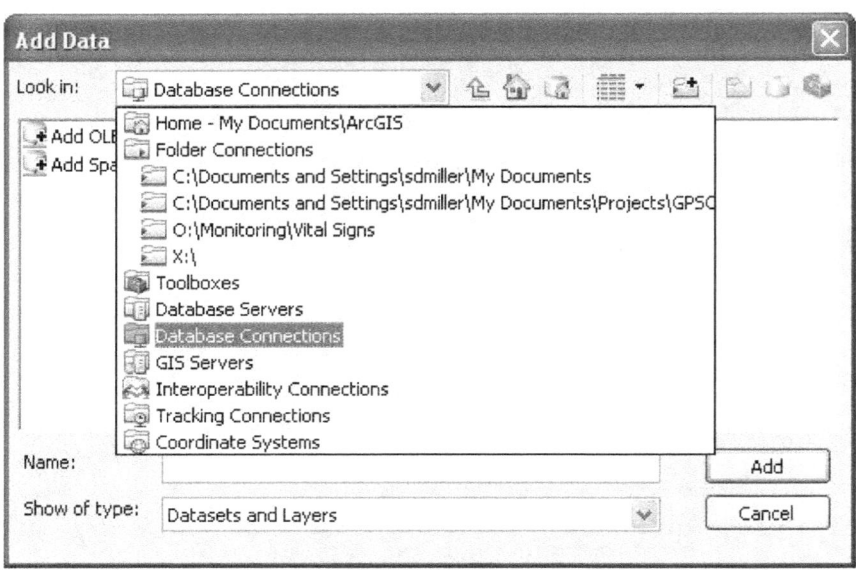

2. The 'Data Link Properties' dialog comes up. Select the appropriate driver for SQL Server.

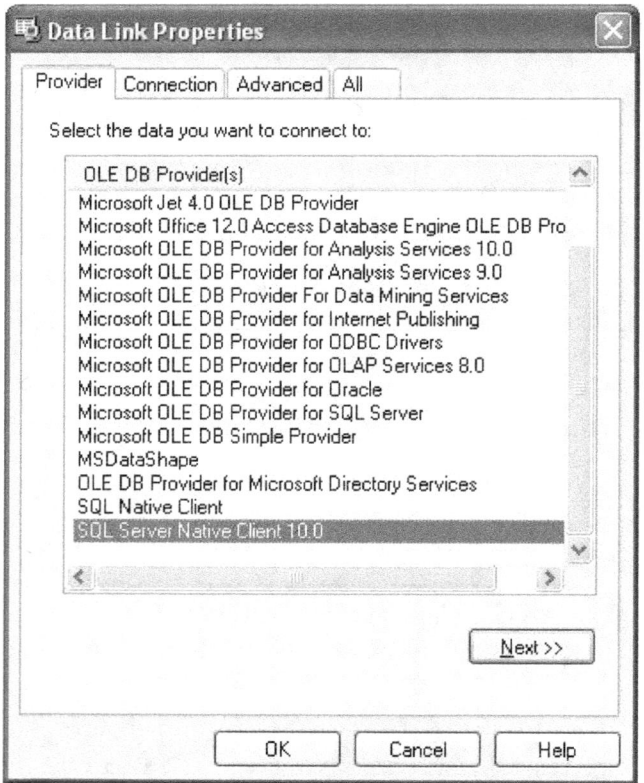

3. The 'Data Link Properties' dialog comes up. Fill in the form according to the screenshot. Click OK.

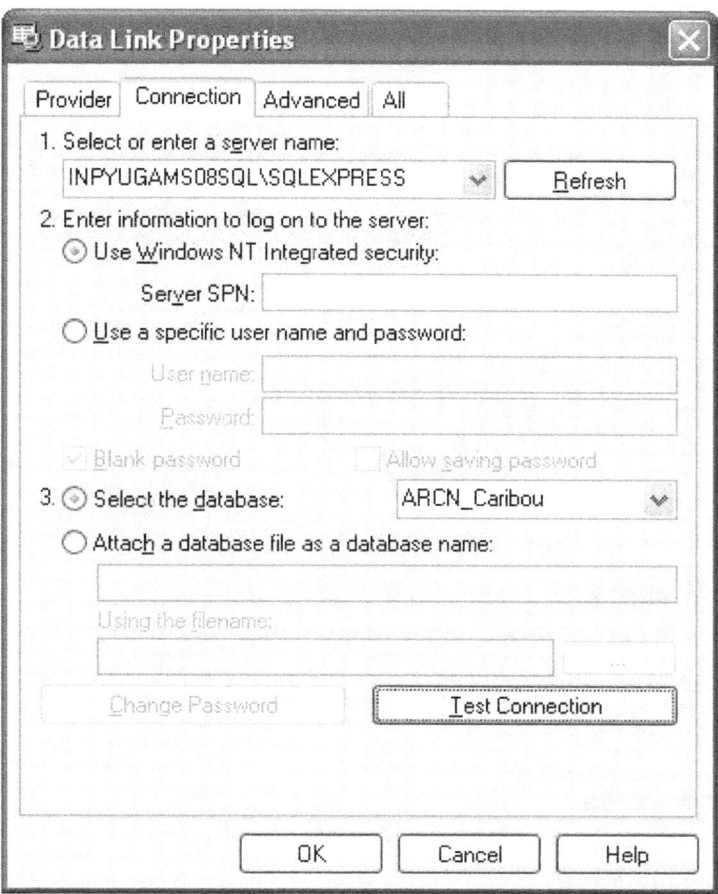

4. Re-name the connection 'ARCN_Caribou' or similar and open the connection.

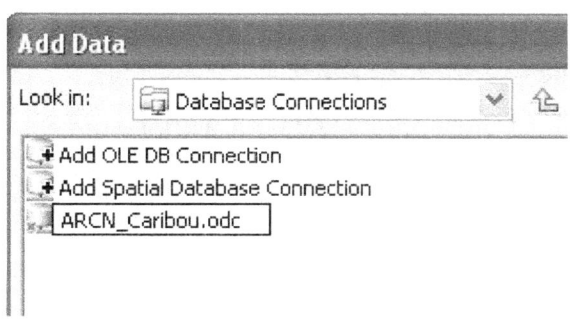

5. Follow the ArcGIS documentation for selecting and adding spatial tables form the database or see 'Exporting GPS Data to ArcGIS' above for an example.

Standard Operating Procedure 11: Generating Metadata for Data Publication

Version 1.0 August, 2012, S.D. Miller

Revision History Log:

Prev. Version #	Revision Date	Author	Changes Made	Reason for Change	New Version #

Scope and Application

Published data must always be accompanied by documentation. This SOP is a continuation of SOP 10 in that it describes how to document the product generated in that SOP with an XML metadata document in Federal Geographic Data Committee (FGDC) format. This format is readily ingested by most Geographic Information Systems as well as the Natural Resource Information Portal.

Materials, Resources and Prerequisites

NPS Metadata Tool and Editor
Data publication shapefile as specified in SOP 10.
Metadata template (optional but recommended, a metadata document from an earlier publication event that can be quickly modified)
Caribou monitoring data conditional use statement (Appendix 5).

How metadata documents and shapefiles work together

A shapefile is not actually one file but a bundle of three or more files all with the same name (but different extensions) in the same directory. A metadata document, if it exists, by convention follows this pattern with a .xml extension. Most GIS software assumes a metadata document will be named the same as the shapefile it describes and therefore looks for 'mydata.xml' after loading 'mydata.shp'. If you use ArcGIS and click the Metadata tab on a layer it looks for a metadata document and if it does not find one it creates one using information it can glean from the data layer such as the coordinate system, projection, data columns and data types. This auto-generated document is not perfect but is a good start. The unfortunate aspect of the auto generated metadata file is that it will overwrite certain fields; fields that you may have spent significant time filling in. A good rule of thumb is to build the metadata document as completely as possible in ArcCatalog and then finish it using the NPS Metadata Tool. For this reason, you should back up your metadata document and/or never utilize the metadata tab in ArcCatalog again.

Generating a Caribou GPS Data Metadata Document

There are two methods for generating a metadata document for the GPS data shapefile. The first method is to simply copy and modify an existing metadata document. The second involves creating a metadata document from scratch.

Copying and updating an existing metadata document

This method is the easiest as most of the fields have been filled in and only a few will need updating such as the metadata creation date, the time period of data coverage etc.

Procedures

1. Copy an existing metadata document from O:\Monitoring\Vital Signs\Caribou\Data\Data Publication to your shapefile directory and rename it the same as your shapefile but with a .xml extension.
2. Open the metadata document using the NPS Metadata Editor.
3. Review the content of the metadata document and edit any fields that need updating referring to the NPS Metadata Tool and Editor documentation for guidance.
4. Ensure that the conditional use statement is included in the metadata.
5. Have the PI review and approve the metadata. A good way to do this is to use the MP parser tool to export the metadata into a more readable html format.
6. Package the shapefile and metadata and any other supporting documentation in a zip archive and archive it at O:\Monitoring\Vital Signs\Caribou\Data\Data Publication

Creating a new metadata document

This method is more time consuming than simply updating an existing metadata document and should be avoided if possible. It involves using ArcCatalog and the NPS Metadata Tools and Editor to build a metadata document. There is no workflow for this method because the documentation within ArcGIS, the NPS Metadata Tools and Editor and the FGDC website are sufficient to accomplish this task.

Standard Operating Procedure 12: Entering caribou data

Version 1.0 August, 2012, S.D. Miller

Revision History Log:

Prev. Version #	Revision Date	Author	Changes Made	Reason for Change	New Version #

Entering caribou capture and calf data (Onion Portage or Net Gun)

Enter caribou capture data as follows:

1. Start the caribou monitoring application (http://165.83.59.7:100/clickonce/caribou/index.htm).
2. Open the main form and select 'Caribou'

3. Click 'Add Caribou'

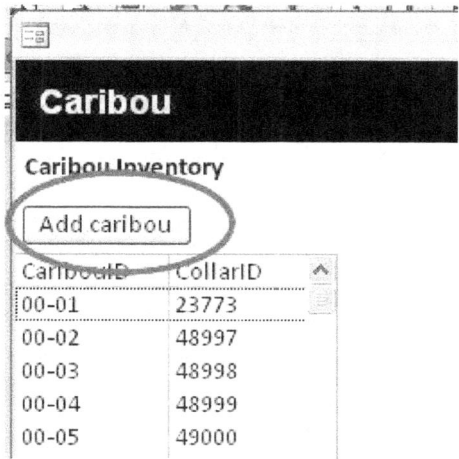

4. The Caribou Detail form appears

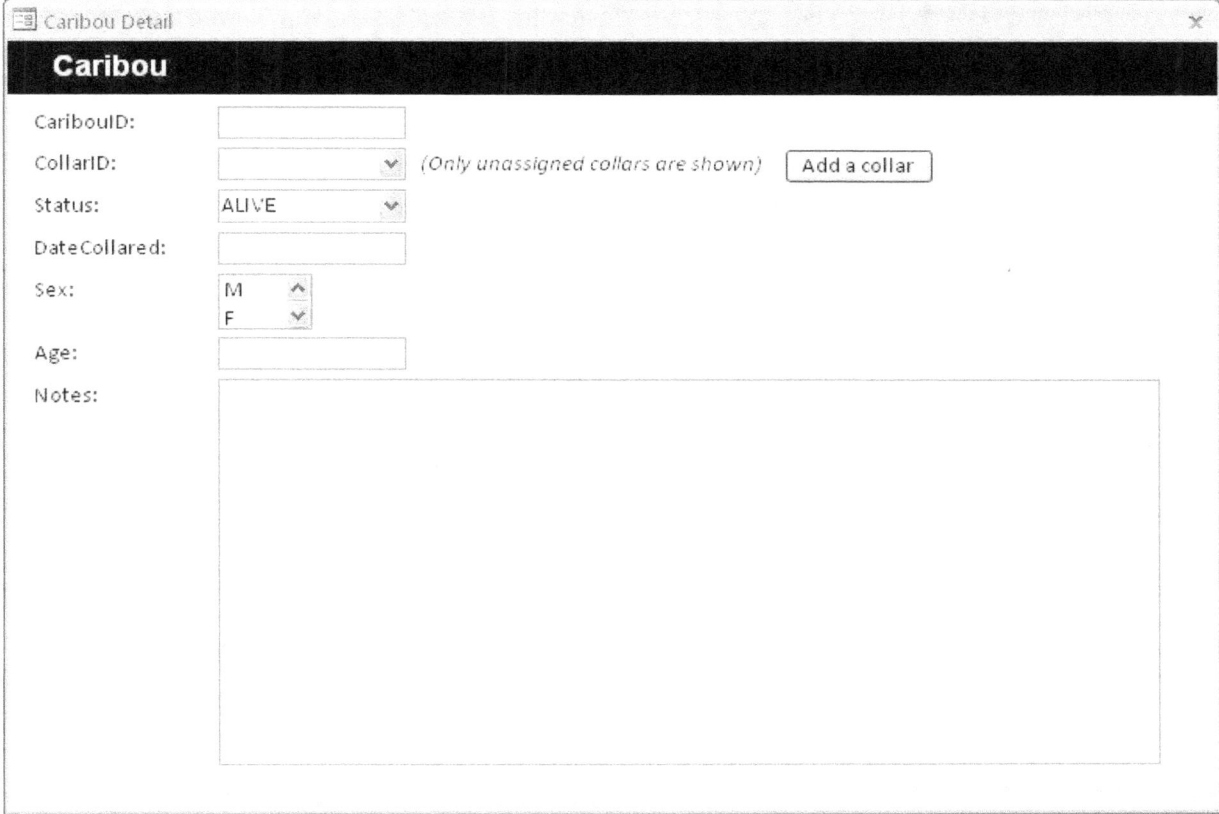

5. Enter the required information and close the form.
6. The new caribou will appear in the caribou inventory on the left side of the Caribou form.

7. Click the 'Capture (Onion Portage)' or 'Capture (Net Gun)' tabs to enter any remaining information about the caribou including calfs.

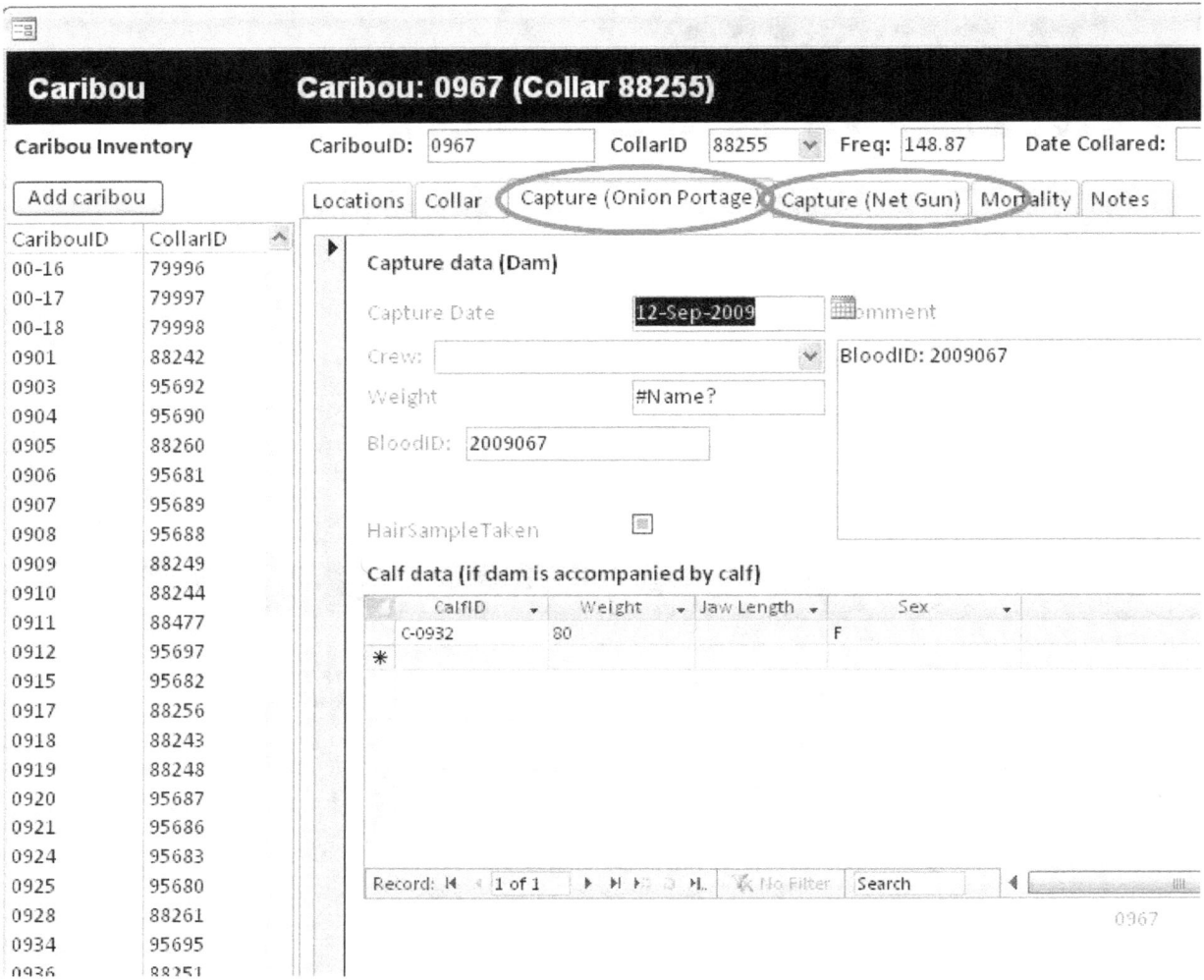

Entering mortality data

Mortality information is entered through the Caribou form by clicking the 'Mortality' tab.

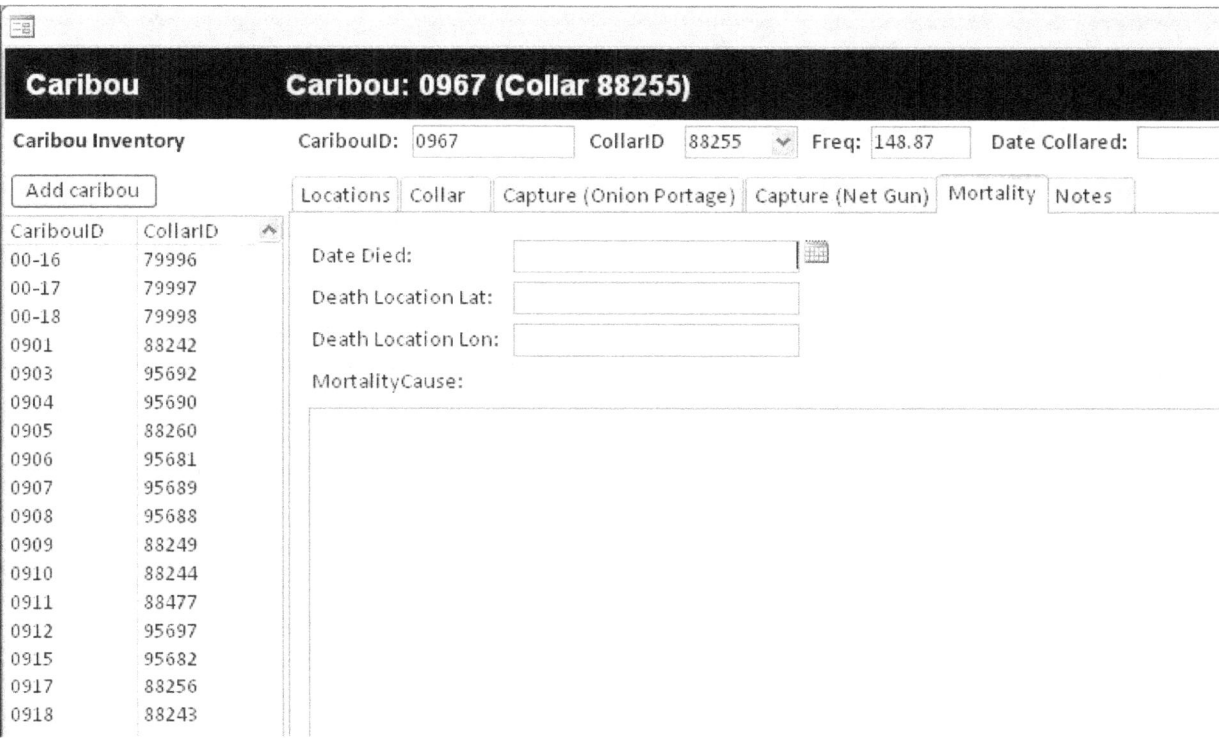

Figure 6. Entering mortality information

Entering collar data

Enter collars through the Collars form.
1. Open the caribou monitoring application (http://165.83.59.7:100/clickonce/caribou/index.htm).
2. Open the main form if it is not open already
3. Click the 'Collar inventory' button

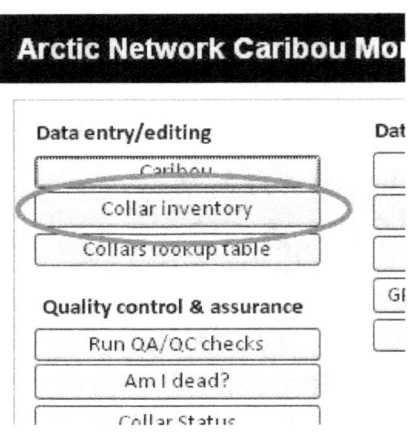

4. The Collars Data Table opens

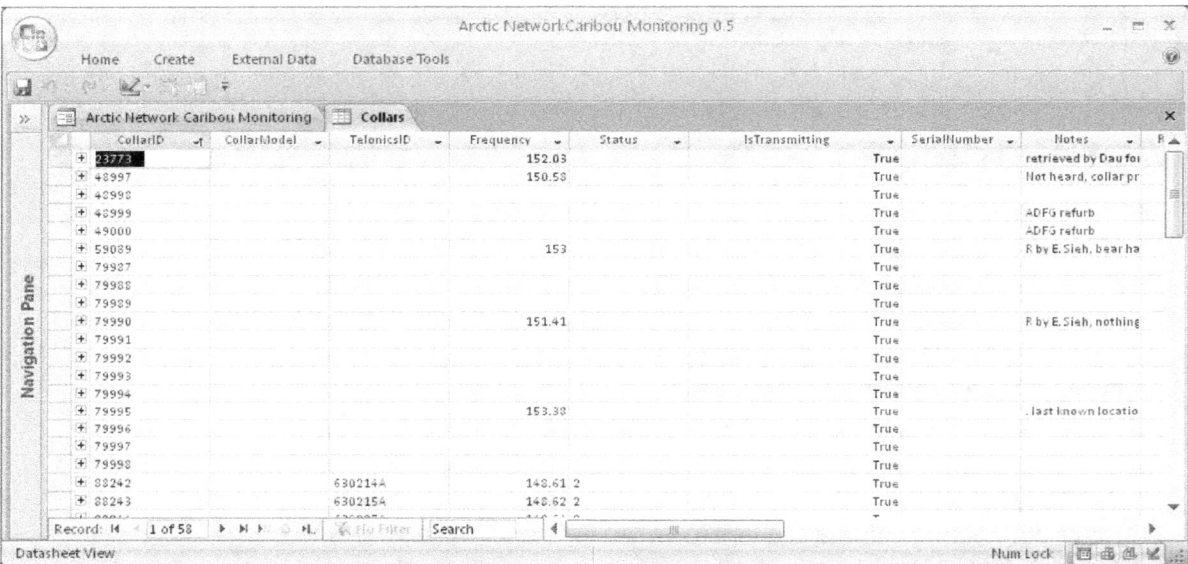

5. Enter the information about the collar into the table.

Standard Operating Procedure 13: Performing Data Quality Control and Assurance Checks

Version 1.0 August, 2012, S.D. Miller

Revision History Log:

Prev. Version #	Revision Date	Author	Changes Made	Reason for Change	New Version #

Scope and Application

The Caribou Monitoring Database (O:\Monitoring\Vital Signs\Caribou\Data\Database) provides robust basic quality control and assurance protections through its design as well as having administrative and programmatic controls. This SOP describes the programmatic quality control measures that can be used to pinpoint errors in the data that should be rectified.

Visual quality control and assurance checks

Systematic and logical errors can be prevented by processes integrated in the database but errors can still creep into the dataset through data entry error, corrupt import files or bad data. There is no substitute for human error checks to detect inconsistencies. The database provides a user interface that allows for easy scanning of data, particularly the spatial data. Errant fixes or fix dates can be easily detected by viewing the data on the screen. The fix dates are color blended from red (old) to green (new) such that a bad date would stand out from its neighbors.

Programmatic quality control and assurance checks

Some logical consistency and range checks are programmed into the Caribou Monitoring Database and Application and others are available as SQL Server scripts.

Application tier data quality checks
Data quality checking algorithms can be accessed through the main form by clicking the 'Run QA\QC checks' button. A form will appear showing the results of basic QA\QC checks (Figure).

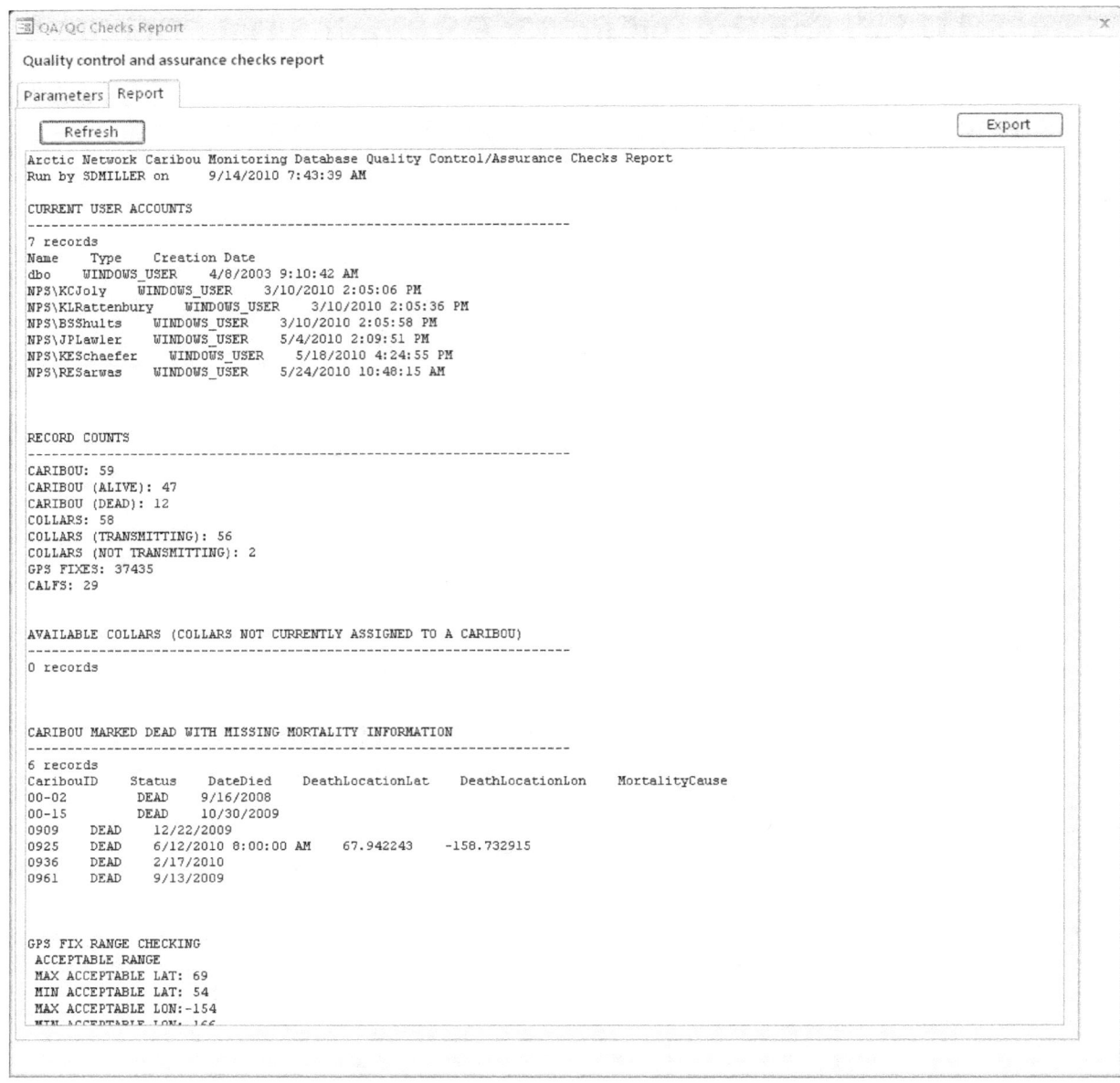

```
QA/QC Checks Report                                                                          x

Quality control and assurance checks report

Parameters  Report

    Refresh                                                                          Export

Arctic Network Caribou Monitoring Database Quality Control/Assurance Checks Report
Run by SDMILLER on      9/14/2010 7:43:39 AM

CURRENT USER ACCOUNTS
-----------------------------------------------------------------------
7 records
Name    Type    Creation Date
dbo     WINDOWS_USER    4/8/2003 9:10:42 AM
NPS\KCJoly    WINDOWS_USER    3/10/2010 2:05:06 PM
NPS\KLRattenbury    WINDOWS_USER    3/10/2010 2:05:36 PM
NPS\BSShults    WINDOWS_USER    3/10/2010 2:05:58 PM
NPS\JPLawler    WINDOWS_USER    5/4/2010 2:09:51 PM
NPS\KESchaefer    WINDOWS_USER    5/18/2010 4:24:55 PM
NPS\RESarwas    WINDOWS_USER    5/24/2010 10:48:15 AM


RECORD COUNTS
-----------------------------------------------------------------------
CARIBOU: 59
CARIBOU (ALIVE): 47
CARIBOU (DEAD): 12
COLLARS: 58
COLLARS (TRANSMITTING): 56
COLLARS (NOT TRANSMITTING): 2
GPS FIXES: 37435
CALFS: 29


AVAILABLE COLLARS (COLLARS NOT CURRENTLY ASSIGNED TO A CARIBOU)
-----------------------------------------------------------------------
0 records


CARIBOU MARKED DEAD WITH MISSING MORTALITY INFORMATION
-----------------------------------------------------------------------
6 records
CaribouID    Status    DateDied    DeathLocationLat    DeathLocationLon    MortalityCause
00-02          DEAD    9/16/2008
00-15          DEAD    10/30/2009
0909    DEAD    12/22/2009
0925    DEAD    6/12/2010 8:00:00 AM    67.942243    -158.732915
0936    DEAD    2/17/2010
0961    DEAD    9/13/2009


GPS FIX RANGE CHECKING
 ACCEPTABLE RANGE
 MAX ACCEPTABLE LAT: 69
 MIN ACCEPTABLE LAT: 54
 MAX ACCEPTABLE LON:-154
 MIN ACCEPTABLE LON: 166
```

Figure 7. Database status, quality control and assurance, logical consistency and range checking.

Database tier data quality checks
A data quality report can be generated by running a SQL script using Microsoft SQL Server Management Studio. See SOP 5 for more information.

Appendix A: Data Model

This appendix details the structure of the database. It is provided here to give an overview of the parameters that are included, its data type (i.e., numeric, text, etc.), restrictions to the data, and the relationship among tables.

Calfs

Database: SQL Server 2008, *Package:* Data Model

Columns

PK	Name	Type	Not Null	Unique	Len	Prec	Scale	Init	Notes
True	CalfID	nvarchar	True	False	50	0	0		0
False	OnionPortageCaptureID	nvarchar	False	False	50	0	0		
False	CaribouID	nvarchar	True	False	50	0	0		0
False	Weight	float	False	False	0	0	0		Calf weight in kilograms
False	Jawlength	float	False	False	0	0	0		Jaw length in cm
False	Sex	nchar	False	False	1	0	0		
False	Comments	nvarchar	False	False	0	0	0		
False	CaptureDate	datetime	False	False	0	0	0		
False	RecordInsertedDate	datetime	False	False	0	0	0	(get date ())	
False	RecordInsertedBy	nvarchar	False	False	50	0	0	(suser_name())	
False	RecordUpdatedDate	datetime	False	False	0	0	0	(get date ())	
False	RecordUpdatedBy	nvarchar	False	False	50	0	0	(suser_name())	
False	RecordCertifiedDate	datetime	False	False	0	0	0		
False	RecordCertifiedBy	nvarchar	False	False	50	0	0		

Constraints

Name	Type	Columns	Initial Code	Notes
PK_ARCNCaribouCalfs	«PK»	CalfID		
FK_ARCNCaribouCalfs	«FK»	OnionPortageCa		

Name	Type	Columns	Initial Code	Notes
_ARCNCaribouCapture Onion		ptureID		
FK_ARCNCaribouCalfs _Mammals	«FK»	CaribouID		

Relationships

Columns	Association		Notes
(OnionPortageCaptureID = OnionPortageCaptureID)	0..*	Calfs.FK_ARCNCaribouCalfs_ARCNCarib ouCaptureOnion	
	1	CaptureOnion. PK_CaptureOnion_1	
(CaribouID = CaribouID)	0..*	Calfs.FK_ARCNCaribouCalfs_Mammals	
	1	Caribou. PK_Mammals	

CaptureNetGun
Database: SQL Server 2008, *Package:* Data Model

Columns

PK	Name	Type	Not Null	Unique	Len	Prec	Scale	Init	Notes
True	NetGunCaptureI D	nvarcha r	True	False	50	0	0		0
False	CaribouID	nvarcha r	False	False	50	0	0		0
False	CaptureDate	datetim e	True	False	0	0	0		0
False	Crew	nvarcha r	False	False	50	0	0		0
False	Weight	float	False	False	0	0	0		0
False	GroupSize	int	False	False	0	0	0		0
False	Lat	decimal	False	False	0	13	8		0
False	Lon	decimal	False	False	0	13	8		0
False	Description	nvarcha r	False	False	255	0	0		0
False	WithCalf	bit	False	False	0	0	0		0
False	IsLactating	bit	False	False	0	0	0		0
False	AntlerPointsLeft	int	False	False	0	0	0		0
False	AntlerPointsRig ht	int	False	False	0	0	0		0
False	AntlerLengthLef t	float	False	False	0	0	0		0
False	AntlerLengthRig ht	float	False	False	0	0	0		0
False	MandibleLength	float	False	False	0	0	0		0
False	NeckCircumfere nce	float	False	False	0	0	0		0

False	MetatarsalLength	float	False	False	0	0	0		0
False	HindFoot	float	False	False	0	0	0		0
False	TotalLength	float	False	False	0	0	0		0
False	HeartGirth	float	False	False	0	0	0		0
False	BodyConditionCode	int	False	False	0	0	0		0
False	WarbleCount	int	False	False	0	0	0		0
False	BodyTemp	float	False	False	0	0	0		0
False	PulseOximeter	float	False	False	0	0	0		0
False	BloodRed	int	False	False	0	0	0		0
False	BloodPurple	int	False	False	0	0	0		0
False	BloodGreen	int	False	False	0	0	0		0
False	ToothTaken	bit	False	False	0	0	0		0
False	HairSampleTaken	bit	False	False	0	0	0		0
False	FecalSampleTaken	bit	False	False	0	0	0		0
False	StartChase	int	False	False	0	0	0		0
False	NumShots	int	False	False	0	0	0		0
False	TimeDown	int	False	False	0	0	0		0
False	Immobilized	int	False	False	0	0	0		0
False	TimeTemp	int	False	False	0	0	0		0
False	Released	int	False	False	0	0	0		0
False	Comments	nvarchar	False	False	0	0	0		0
False	RecordInsertedDate	datetime	False	False	0	0	0	(getdate())	
False	RecordInsertedBy	nvarchar	False	False	50	0	0	(suser_name())	
False	RecordUpdatedDate	datetime	False	False	0	0	0	(getdate())	
False	RecordUpdatedBy	nvarchar	False	False	50	0	0	(suser_name())	
False	RecordCertifiedDate	datetime	False	False	0	0	0		
False	RecordCertifiedBy	nvarchar	False	False	50	0	0		

Name	Type	Columns	Initial Code	Notes
PK_CaptureNetGun	«PK»	NetGunCaptureID		
FK_ARCNCaribouCaptureNetGun_Mammals	«FK»	CaribouID		

Relationships

Columns	Association	Notes
(CaribouID = CaribouID)	0..* CaptureNetGun.FK_ARCNCaribouCaptureNetGun_Mammals 1 Caribou. PK_Mammals	

CaptureOnion

Database: SQL Server 2008, *Package:* Data Model

Columns

PK	Name	Type	Not Null	Unique	Len	Prec	Scale	Init	Notes
True	OnionPortageCaptureID	nvarchar	True	False	50	0	0		0
False	CaribouID	nvarchar	False	False	50	0	0		0
False	CaptureDate	datetime	True	False	0	0	0		0
False	Crew	nvarchar	False	False	50	0	0		0
False	BloodID	nvarchar	False	False	50	0	0		ID of the blood sample
False	HairSampleTaken	bit	False	False	0	0	0		0
False	Comment	nvarchar	False	False	0	0	0		0
False	RecordCreationDate	datetime	True	False	0	0	0	(get date ())	0
False	RecordUpdated	datetime	False	False	0	0	0		0
False	RecordInsertedDate	datetime	False	False	0	0	0	(get date ())	
False	RecordInsertedBy	nvarchar	False	False	50	0	0	(suser_name())	
False	RecordUpdatedD	datetime	False	False	0	0	0	(get	

	ate	e						date ())	
False	RecordUpdatedB y	nvarcha r	False	False	50	0	0	(sus er_ nam e())	
False	RecordCertified Date	datetim e	False	False	0	0	0		
False	RecordCertified By	nvarcha r	False	False	50	0	0		

Constraints

Name	Type	Columns	Initial Code	Notes
PK_CaptureOnion_1	«PK»	OnionPortageCa ptureID		
FK_ARCNCaribouCapt ureOnion_Mammals	«FK»	CaribouID		

Relationships

Columns	Association	Notes
(OnionPortageCaptureID = OnionPortageCaptureID)	**0..*** Calfs.**FK_ARCNCaribouCalfs_ARCNCarib** ouCaptureOnion **1** CaptureOnion. PK_CaptureOnion_1	
(CaribouID = CaribouID)	**0..*** CaptureOnion.**FK_ARCNCaribouCaptureO** nion_Mammals **1** Caribou. PK_Mammals	

Caribou

Database: SQL Server 2008, *Package:* Data Model

Columns

PK	Name	Type	Not Null	Unique	Len	Prec	Scale	Init	Notes
True	CaribouID	nvarcha r	True	False	50	0	0		0
False	CollarID	nvarcha r	False	False	100	0	0		0
False	Status	nvarcha r	False	False	50	0	0		0
False	DateCollared	datetim e	False	False	0	0	0		0
False	Sex	nchar	False	False	1	0	0		0
False	Age	int	False	False	0	0	0		0
False	Notes	ntext	False	False	0	0	0		0
False	FateCause	nvarcha	False	False	50	0	0		0

		r							
False	DateDied	datetime	False	False	0	0	0		0
False	DeathLocationLat	decimal	False	False	0	13	8		0
False	DeathLocationLon	decimal	False	False	0	13	8		0
False	MortalityCause	nvarchar	False	False	50	0	0		0
False	RecordInsertedDate	datetime	False	False	0	0	0	(get date ())	0
False	RecordInsertedBy	nvarchar	False	False	50	0	0	(suser_name())	0
False	RecordUpdatedDate	datetime	False	False	0	0	0	(get date ())	0
False	RecordUpdatedBy	nvarchar	False	False	50	0	0	(suser_name())	0
False	RecordCertified Date	datetime	False	False	0	0	0		0
False	RecordCertified By	nvarchar	False	False	50	0	0		0

Constraints

Name	Type	Columns	Initial Code	Notes
PK_Mammals	«PK»	CaribouID		
FK_Mammals_Collars	«FK»	CollarID		

Relationships

Columns	Association		Notes
(CaribouID = CaribouID)	0..*	Calfs.FK_ARCNCaribouCalfs_Mammals	
	1	Caribou. PK_Mammals	
(CaribouID = CaribouID)	0..*	CaptureNetGun.FK_ARCNCaribouCaptureNetGun_Mammals	
	1	Caribou. PK_Mammals	
(CaribouID = CaribouID)	0..*	CaptureOnion.FK_ARCNCaribouCaptureOnion_Mammals	
	1	Caribou. PK_Mammals	
(CollarID = CollarID)	0..*	Caribou.FK_Mammals_Collars	
	1	Collars. PK_Collars	

78

Columns	Association	Notes
(CaribouID = CaribouID)	**0..*** CaribouLocations.**FK_MammalLocations_** Mammals **1** Caribou. **PK_Mammals**	
(CaribouID = CaribouID)	**0..*** CaribouLocationsPTT.**FK_CaribouLocation** sPTT_Caribou **1** Caribou. **PK_Mammals**	

CaribouLocations

Database: SQL Server 2008, *Package:* Data Model

Columns

PK	Name	Type	Not Null	Unique	Len	Prec	Scale	Init	Notes
True	CaribouID	nvarchar	True	False	50	0	0		0
True	FixDate	datetime	True	False	0	0	0		0
False	FixDateAST	datetime	False	False	0	0	0		
False	JulianDay	int	False	False	0	0	0		
False	Lat	decimal	True	False	0	18	8		0
False	Lon	decimal	True	False	0	18	8		0
False	Temperature	float	False	False	0	0	0		0
False	Workbook	nvarchar	True	False	255	0	0		0
False	SegmentDistance	decimal	False	False	0	8	3		
False	SegmentTime	int	False	False	0	0	0		
False	RecordInsertedDate	datetime	False	False	0	0	0	(get date ())	0
False	RecordInsertedBy	nvarchar	False	False	50	0	0	(sus er_ nam e())	0
False	RecordUpdatedDate	datetime	False	False	0	0	0	(get date ())	0
False	RecordUpdatedBy	nvarchar	False	False	50	0	0	(sus er_ nam e())	0
False	RecordCertifiedDate	datetime	False	False	0	0	0		0

False	RecordCertified By	nvarchar	False	False	50	0	0	0

Constraints

Name	Type	Columns	Initial Code	Notes
PK_CaribouLocations	«PK»	CaribouIDFixDate		
FK_MammalLocations_ Mammals	«FK»	CaribouID		

Relationships

Columns	Association	Notes
(CaribouID = CaribouID)	0..* CaribouLocations.FK_MammalLocations_ Mammals 1 Caribou. PK_Mammals	

CaribouLocationsPTT

Database: SQL Server 2008, *Package:* Data Model

Columns

PK	Name	Type	Not Null	Unique	Len	Prec	Scale	Init	Notes
True	CaribouID	nvarchar	True	False	50	0	0		
True	FixDate	datetime	True	False	0	0	0		
False	FixDateAST	datetime	False	False	0	0	0		
False	LocationClass	int	False	False	0	0	0		
False	Lat	decimal	True	False	0	18	8		
False	Lon	decimal	True	False	0	18	8		
False	Workbook	nvarchar	True	False	255	0	0		
False	RecordInsertedDate	datetime	False	False	0	0	0	(get date ())	
False	RecordInsertedBy	nvarchar	False	False	50	0	0	(suser_ name())	
False	RecordUpdatedDate	datetime	False	False	0	0	0	(get date ())	
False	RecordUpdatedBy	nvarchar	False	False	50	0	0	(suser_ nam	

False	RecordCertified Date	datetime	False	False	0	0	0	e())	
False	RecordCertified By	nvarchar	False	False	50	0	0		

Constraints

Name	Type	Columns	Initial Code	Notes
PK_CaribouLocationsPTT	«PK»	CaribouIDFixDate		
FK_CaribouLocationsPTT_Caribou	«FK»	CaribouID		

Relationships

Columns	Association	Notes
(CaribouID = CaribouID)	0..* CaribouLocationsPTT.FK_CaribouLocationsPTT_Caribou 1 Caribou. PK_Mammals	

CaribouSurveys

Database: SQL Server 2008, *Package:* Data Model

Columns

PK	Name	Type	Not Null	Unique	Len	Prec	Scale	Init	Notes
True	CaribouSurveyID	nvarchar	True	False	50	0	0		Primary key. Synthetic or natural. Required. A string that distinguishes this record from all others.
False	SurveyID	nvarchar	True	False	50	0	0		Foreign key to Surveys table
False	MammalID	nvarchar	False	False	50	0	0		MammalID, if known
False	SightingTime	datetime	True	False	0	0	0		Time of sighting
False	GroupNumber	int	True	False	0	0	0		Group number
False	CalfAtHeel	bit	False	False	0	0	0		Was there a calf at heel (T/F)
False	NumberOfAntlers	int	False	False	0	0	0		Number of antlers (1;2)
False	AntlerStatus	nchar	False	False	1	0	0		Antler status (H;V;N) H=Hard,

									V=Velvet, N=None
False	Udder	nchar	False	False	1	0	0		Udder condition (D;N) D=Distended, N=Not distended.
False	Lat	decimal	False	False	0	13	8		Latitude in geographic coordinates WGS84
False	Lon	decimal	False	False	0	13	8		Longitude in geographic coordinates WGS84
False	Comment	nvarchar	False	False	0	0	0		Comments
False	RecordInsertedDate	datetime	False	False	0	0	0	(get date ())	
False	RecordInsertedBy	nvarchar	False	False	50	0	0	(suser_name())	
False	RecordUpdatedDate	datetime	False	False	0	0	0	(get date ())	
False	RecordUpdatedBy	nvarchar	False	False	50	0	0	(suser_name())	
False	RecordCertifiedDate	datetime	False	False	0	0	0		
False	RecordCertifiedBy	nvarchar	False	False	50	0	0		

Constraints

Name	Type	Columns	Initial Code	Notes
PK_ARCNCaribouCalfSurveys	«PK»	CaribouSurveyID		
FK_ARCNCaribouCalfSurveys_tblSurveys	«FK»	SurveyID		

Relationships

Columns	Association	Notes
(SurveyID = SurveyID)	0..* CaribouSurveys.FK_ARCNCaribouCalfSurveys_tblSurveys	

Columns		Association	Notes
	1	Surveys. PK_tblSurveys	

Collars

Database: SQL Server 2008, *Package:* Data Model

Columns

PK	Name	Type	Not Null	Unique	Len	Prec	Scale	Init	Notes
True	CollarID	nvarchar	True	False	100	0	0		0
False	TelonicsID	nvarchar	False	False	100	0	0		0
False	Frequency	decimal	False	False	0	18	3		0
False	Status	nvarchar	False	False	20	0	0		0
False	IsTransmitting	bit	False	False	0	0	0		0
False	Notes	nvarchar	False	False	0	0	0		0
False	SerialNumber	nvarchar	False	False	255	0	0		0
False	CollarModel	nvarchar	False	False	50	0	0		0
False	RecordInsertedDate	datetime	False	False	0	0	0	(getdate())	0
False	RecordInsertedBy	nvarchar	False	False	50	0	0	(suser_name())	0
False	RecordUpdatedDate	datetime	False	False	0	0	0	(getdate())	0
False	RecordUpdatedBy	nvarchar	False	False	50	0	0	(suser_name())	0
False	CollarLocation	nvarchar	False	False	50	0	0		0
False	DateRetrieved	nvarchar	False	False	50	0	0		0

Constraints

Name	Type	Columns	Initial Code	Notes
PK_Collars	«PK»	CollarID		

Columns	Association		Notes
(CollarID = CollarID)	**0..***	Caribou.FK_Mammals_Collars	
	1	Collars. PK_Collars	

Surveys

Database: SQL Server 2008, *Package:* Data Model

Columns

PK	Name	Type	Not Null	Unique	Len	Prec	Scale	Init	Notes
True	SurveyID	nvarchar	True	False	50	0	0		User defined ID for the survey. May be observer name, survey location, tail number, user defined naming scheme, etc., that helps distinguish this survey from all the others. Required
False	MammalType	nvarchar	True	False	20	0	0		Mammal survey type (Moose, Caribou, Brown Bear, etc.). Required.
False	SurveyDate	smalldatetime	True	False	0	0	0		Date of the survey. Required
False	Location	nchar	True	False	255	0	0		Location of the survey
False	IsComplete	bit	False	False	0	0	0		Was the survey completed? False if the survey was abandoned due to bad weather or other factors.
False	Pilot	nvarchar	True	False	20	0	0		Survey pilot
False	Observer	nvarchar	True	False	20	0	0		Observer
False	AircraftType	nvarchar	False	False	50	0	0		Aircraft used during the survey.
False	TailNo	nvarchar	False	False	50	0	0		Aircraft tail number.
False	CloudCover	nvarchar	False	False	50	0	0		

		r							
False	Precipitation	nvarchar	False	False	50	0	0		
False	Turbulence	nvarchar	False	False	50	0	0		
False	LightIntensity	nvarchar	False	False	50	0	0		
False	ElapsedTime_Min	int	False	False	0	0	0		Total flight time in minutes. Only tally actual surveying time, not potty breaks, weather breaks, etc.
False	ProtocolVersion	decimal	False	False	0	4	1		
False	IsCertified	bit	False	False	0	0	0		Is the data for this survey certified for publication and distribution
False	TripReport	nvarchar	False	False	0	0	0		
False	Comments	nvarchar	False	False	0	0	0		
False	RecordCreatedBy	nvarchar	True	False	50	0	0	(suser_name())	
False	RecordCreationDate	datetime	True	False	0	0	0	(getdate())	
False	UpdatedBy	nvarchar	False	False	50	0	0		
False	UpdatedDate	datetime	False	False	0	0	0		
False	VerifiedBy	nvarchar	False	False	50	0	0		
False	VerifiedDate	datetime	False	False	0	0	0		
False	RecordInsertedDate	datetime	False	False	0	0	0	(getdate())	
False	RecordInsertedBy	nvarchar	False	False	50	0	0	(suser_name())	
False	RecordUpdatedD	datetime	False	False	0	0	0	(get	

	ate	e							date	
									(())	
False	RecordUpdatedBy	nvarchar	False	False	50	0	0	(suser_name())	
False	RecordCertifiedDate	datetime	False	False	0	0	0		
False	RecordCertifiedBy	nvarchar	False	False	50	0	0		

Constraints

Name	Type	Columns	Initial Code	Notes
PK_tblSurveys	«PK»	SurveyID		

Relationships

Columns	Association	Notes
(SurveyID = SurveyID)	0..* CaribouSurveys.FK_ARCNCaribouCalfSurveys_tblSurveys 1 Surveys. PK_tblSurveys	

tbl_DB_Meta

Database: SQL Server 2008, *Package:* Data Model

Columns

PK	Name	Type	Not Null	Unique	Len	Prec	Scale	Init	Notes
True	DB_Meta_ID	nvarchar	True	False	50	0	0	(newid())	0
False	Meta_MID	nvarchar	False	False	50	0	0		0
False	Dcat_ID	nvarchar	False	False	50	0	0		0
False	DatabaseName	nvarchar	True	False	50	0	0		0

Constraints

Name	Type	Columns	Initial Code	Notes
PK_tbl_DB_Meta	«PK»	DB_Meta_ID		

Relationships

Columns	Association	Notes
(DB_Meta_ID = DB_Meta_ID)	0..* tbl_DB_Revisions.FK_tbl_DB_Revisions_tbl_DB_Meta 1 tbl_DB_Meta. PK_tbl_DB_Meta	

tbl_DB_Revisions

Database: SQL Server 2008, *Package:* Data Model

Columns

PK	Name	Type	Not Null	Unique	Len	Prec	Scale	Init	Notes
True	Revision_ID	nvarchar	True	False	50	0	0	(newid())	0
False	DB_Meta_ID	nvarchar	True	False	50	0	0	(N'C894CB4B-7CEA-4006-860E-9462B9DF37ED')	0
False	Revision_Date	smalldatetime	True	False	0	0	0	(getdate())	0
False	Revision_By	nvarchar	True	False	50	0	0	(suser_name())	0
False	Revision_Reason	nvarchar	True	False	255	0	0		0
False	Revision_Description	nvarchar	False	False	2000	0	0		0
False	DatabaseVersion	decimal	True	False	0	18	2		0

Constraints

Name	Type	Columns	Initial Code	Notes
PK_tbl_DB_Revisions	«PK»	Revision_ID		
FK_tbl_DB_Revisions_tbl_DB_Meta	«FK»	DB_Meta_ID		

Columns	Association	Notes
(DB_Meta_ID = DB_Meta_ID)	**0..*** tbl_DB_Revisions.FK_tbl_DB_Revisions_tbl_DB_Meta **1** tbl_DB_Meta. PK_tbl_DB_Meta	

tluCollarModels

Database: SQL Server 2008, *Package:* Data Model

Columns

PK	Name	Type	Not Null	Unique	Len	Prec	Scale	Init	Notes
True	CollarModel	nvarchar	True	False	50	0	0		0
False	Weight	float	True	False	0	0	0		0

Constraints

Name	Type	Columns	Initial Code	Notes
PK_tluCollarModels	«PK»	CollarModel		

Requirements

Type:	**Package**
Package:	Arctic Network Caribou Monitoring
Detail:	*Created on* 9/2/2010 11:25:33 AM. *Last modified on* 9/2/2010 11:25:33 AM
Notes:	

Requirements

Created By: on 9/2/2010
Last Modified: 9/2/2010, *Version:* 1.0

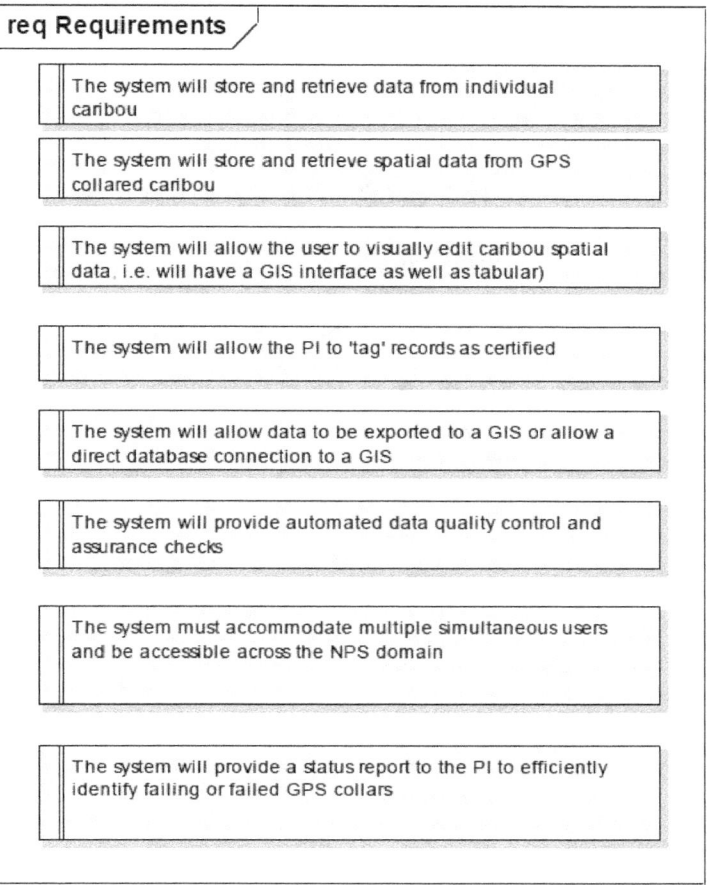

req Requirements

The system will store and retrieve data from individual caribou

The system will store and retrieve spatial data from GPS collared caribou

The system will allow the user to visually edit caribou spatial data, i.e. will have a GIS interface as well as tabular)

The system will allow the PI to 'tag' records as certified

The system will allow data to be exported to a GIS or allow a direct database connection to a GIS

The system will provide automated data quality control and assurance checks

The system must accommodate multiple simultaneous users and be accessible across the NPS domain

The system will provide a status report to the PI to efficiently identify failing or failed GPS collars

Requirement1
Database: <none>, *Package:* Requirements
Detail: Created on 9/2/2010. Last modified on.9/2/2010.
Notes:

The system must accommodate multiple simultaneous users and be accessible across the NPS domain
Database: <none>, *Package:* Requirements
Detail: Created on 9/2/2010. Last modified on.9/2/2010.
Notes:

The system will allow data to be exported to a GIS or allow a direct database connection to a GIS
Database: <none>, *Package:* Requirements
Detail: Created on 9/2/2010. Last modified on.9/2/2010.
Notes: The system must be accessible by ESRI ArcGIS software for data analysis since the vast majority of data analysis will be spatial in nature.

The system will allow the PI to 'tag' records as certified
Database: <none>, *Package:* Requirements
Detail: Created on 9/2/2010. Last modified on.9/2/2010.
Notes:

The system will allow the user to visually edit caribou spatial data, i.e. will have a GIS interface as well as tabular)
Database: <none>, *Package:* Requirements
Detail: Created on 9/2/2010. Last modified on.9/2/2010.
Notes:

The system will provide a status report to the PI to efficiently identify failing or failed GPS collars
Database: <none>, *Package:* Requirements
Detail: Created on 9/2/2010. Last modified on.9/2/2010.
Notes:

The system will provide automated data quality control and assurance checks
Database: <none>, *Package:* Requirements
Detail: Created on 9/2/2010. Last modified on.9/2/2010.
Notes:

The system will store and retrieve data from individual caribou
Database: <none>, *Package:* Requirements
Detail: Created on 9/2/2010. Last modified on.9/2/2010.
Notes:

The system will store and retrieve spatial data from GPS collared caribou
Database: <none>, *Package:* Requirements
Detail: Created on 9/2/2010. Last modified on.9/2/2010.
Notes:

Deployment
Type: **Package**
Package: Arctic Network Caribou Monitoring
Detail: Created on 8/26/2010 10:28:09 AM. Last modified on 8/26/2010 10:28:09 AM
Notes:

Deployment
Created By: on 8/26/2010
Last Modified: 8/26/2010, *Version:*1.0

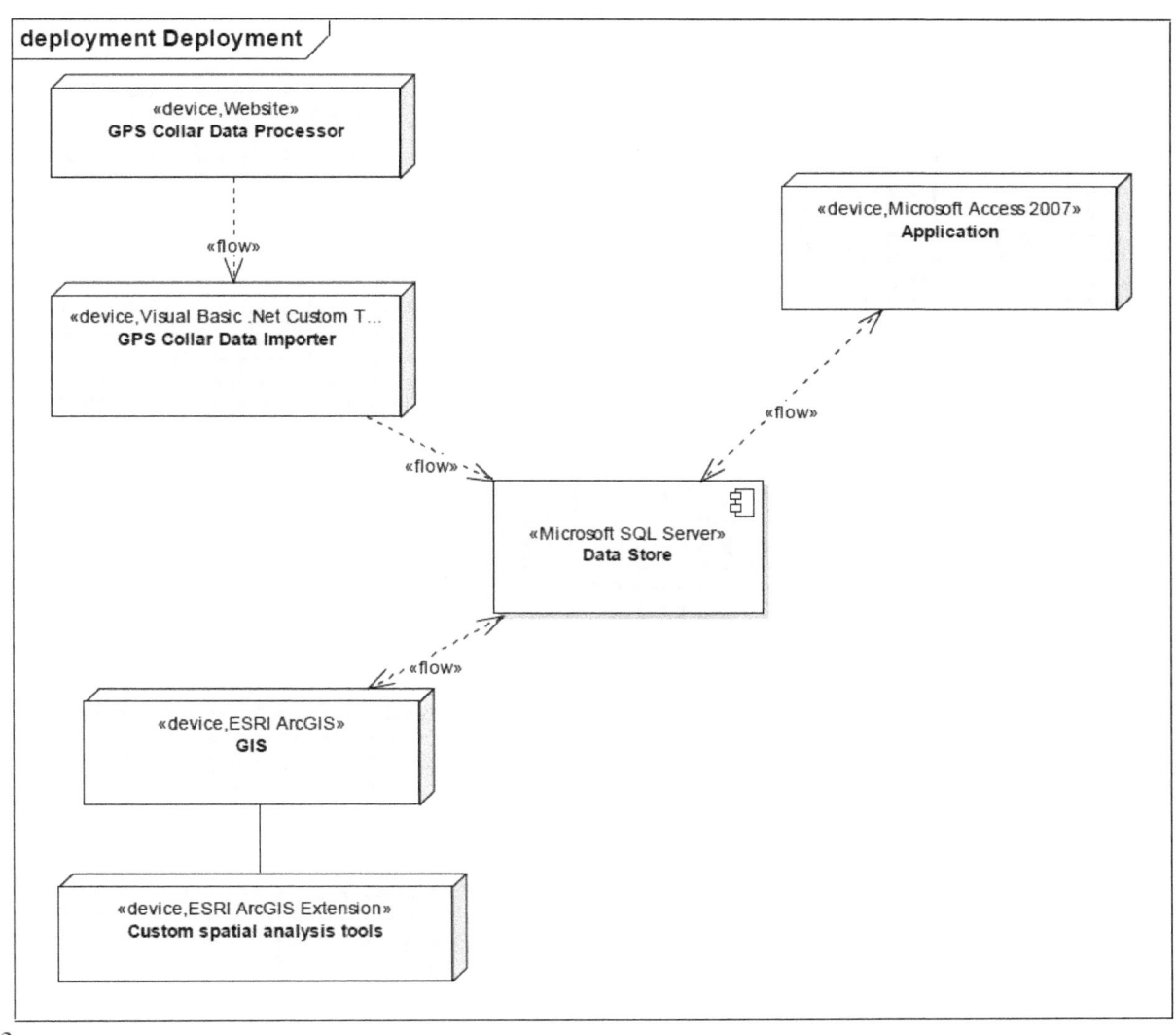

3

Data Store

Database: Java, *Package:* Deployment

Detail: Created on 8/26/2010. Last modified on.8/26/2010.

Notes:

Columns	Association	Notes
	GPS Collar Data Importer. Data Store.	
	Application. Data Store.	
	GIS. Data Store.	

Application

Database:	Java, *Package:* Deployment	
Detail:	*Created on* 8/26/2010. *Last modified on.*8/26/2010.	
Notes:		

Columns	Association	Notes
	Application. Data Store.	

Custom spatial analysis tools

Database:	Java, *Package:* Deployment	
Detail:	*Created on* 8/26/2010. *Last modified on.*8/26/2010.	
Notes:		

Columns	Association	Notes
	GIS. Custom spatial analysis tools.	

GIS

Database:	Java, *Package:* Deployment	
Detail:	*Created on* 8/26/2010. *Last modified on.*8/26/2010.	
Notes:		

Columns	Association	Notes
	GIS. Custom spatial analysis tools.	
	GIS. Data Store.	

GPS Collar Data Importer

Database:	Java, *Package:* Deployment	
Detail:	*Created on* 8/26/2010. *Last modified on.*8/26/2010.	
Notes:		

Relationships

Columns	Association	Notes
	GPS Collar Data Importer. Data Store.	
	GPS Collar Data Processor. GPS Collar Data Importer.	

GPS Collar Data Processor

Database: Java, *Package:* Deployment

Detail: Created on 8/26/2010. Last modified on 8/26/2010.

Notes:

Relationships

Columns	Association	Notes
	GPS Collar Data Processor. GPS Collar Data Importer.	

Use Cases

Type: **Package**

Package: Arctic Network Caribou Monitoring

Detail: Created on 8/26/2010 10:18:47 AM. Last modified on 8/26/2010 10:18:47 AM

Notes:

Biotechnician

Created By: on 8/26/2010

Last Modified: 8/26/2010, *Version:*1.0

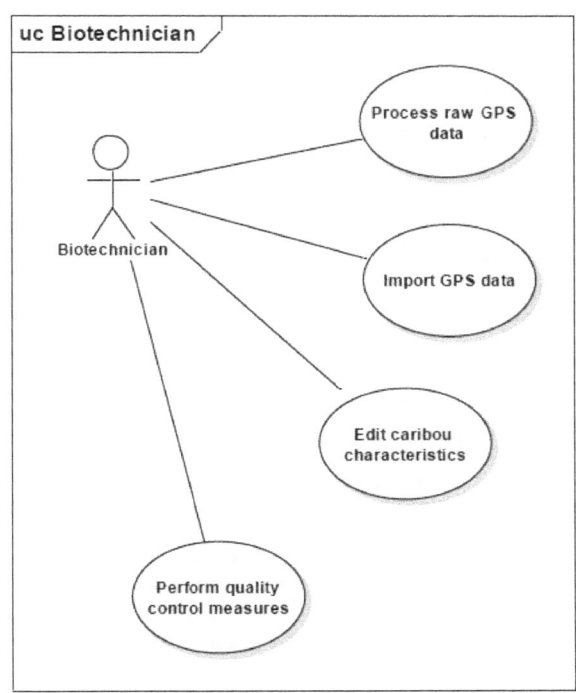

Data Manager

Created By: on 8/26/2010
Last Modified: 8/26/2010, *Version:* 1.0

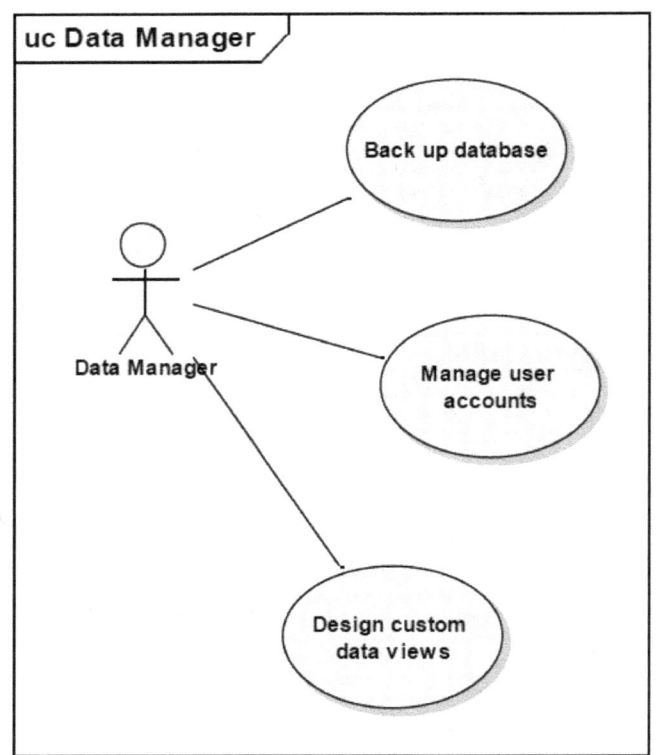

Principal Investigator

Created By: on 8/26/2010
Last Modified: 8/26/2010, *Version:*1.0

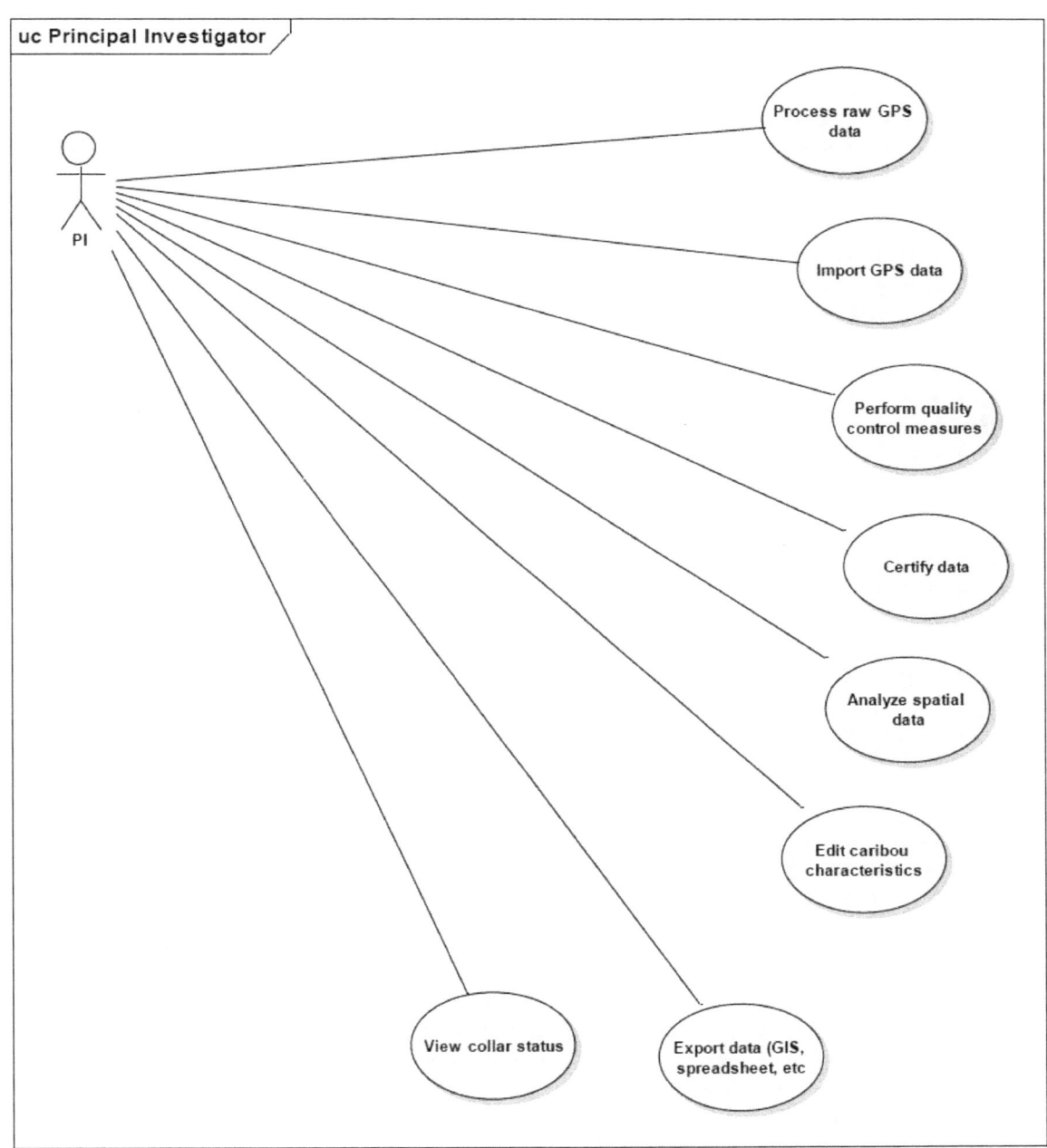

Biotechnician
Database: <none>, *Package:* Use Cases
Detail: *Created on 8/26/2010. Last modified on.8/26/2010.*
Notes:

Columns	Association	Notes
	Biotechnician. Process raw GPS data.	
	Biotechnician. Import GPS data.	
	Biotechnician. Edit caribou characteristics.	
	Biotechnician. Perform quality control measures.	

Data Manager

Database:	\<none\>, *Package:* Use Cases	
Detail:	*Created on 8/26/2010. Last modified on.8/26/2010.*	
Notes:		

Relationships

Columns	Association	Notes
	Data Manager. Back up database.	
	Data Manager. Manage user accounts.	
	Data Manager. Design custom data views.	

PI

Database:	\<none\>, *Package:* Use Cases	
Detail:	*Created on 8/26/2010. Last modified on.8/26/2010.*	
Notes:		

Relationships

Columns	Association	Notes
	PI. Import GPS data.	
	PI. Perform quality control measures.	
	PI. Certify data.	
	PI. Analyze spatial data.	
	PI. Edit caribou characteristics.	
	PI. Export data (GIS, spreadsheet, etc.	
	PI. View collar status.	

Columns	Association	Notes
	PI. Process raw GPS data.	

Analyze spatial data

Database: <none>, *Package:* Use Cases

Detail: Created on 8/26/2010. Last modified on.8/26/2010.

Notes:

Relationships

Columns	Association	Notes
	PI. Analyze spatial data.	

Back up database

Database: <none>, *Package:* Use Cases

Detail: Created on 8/26/2010. Last modified on.8/26/2010.

Notes:

Relationships

Columns	Association	Notes
	Data Manager. Back up database.	

Certify data

Database: <none>, *Package:* Use Cases

Detail: Created on 8/26/2010. Last modified on.8/26/2010.

Notes:

Relationships

Columns	Association	Notes
	PI. Certify data.	

Design custom data views

Database: <none>, *Package:* Use Cases

Detail: Created on 8/26/2010. Last modified on.8/26/2010.

Notes:

Relationships

Columns	Association	Notes
	Data Manager. Design custom data views.	

Edit caribou characteristics

Database: <none>, *Package:* Use Cases

Detail: Created on 8/26/2010. Last modified on.8/26/2010.

Notes:

Columns	Association	Notes
	PI. Edit caribou characteristics.	
	Biotechnician. Edit caribou characteristics.	

Export data (GIS, spreadsheet, etc

Database: <none>, *Package:* Use Cases

Detail: *Created on 8/26/2010. Last modified on.8/26/2010.*

Notes:

Relationships

Columns	Association	Notes
	PI. Export data (GIS, spreadsheet, etc.	

Import GPS data

Database: <none>, *Package:* Use Cases

Detail: *Created on 8/26/2010. Last modified on.8/26/2010.*

Notes:

Relationships

Columns	Association	Notes
	PI. Import GPS data.	
	Biotechnician. Import GPS data.	

Manage user accounts

Database: <none>, *Package:* Use Cases

Detail: *Created on 8/26/2010. Last modified on.8/26/2010.*

Notes:

Relationships

Columns	Association	Notes
	Data Manager. Manage user accounts.	

Perform quality control measures

Database: <none>, *Package:* Use Cases

Detail: *Created on 8/26/2010. Last modified on.8/26/2010.*

Notes:

Columns	Association	Notes
	PI. Perform quality control measures.	
	Biotechnician. Perform quality control measures.	

Process raw GPS data

Database: <none>, *Package:* Use Cases

Detail: *Created on 8/26/2010. Last modified on.8/26/2010.*

Notes:

Relationships

Columns	Association	Notes
	Biotechnician. Process raw GPS data.	
	PI. Process raw GPS data.	

View collar status

Database: <none>, *Package:* Use Cases

Detail: *Created on 8/26/2010. Last modified on.8/26/2010.*

Notes: The PI must be able to quickly determine if collars have become disabled, when they last broadcasted.

Relationships

Columns	Association	Notes
	PI. View collar status.	

NPS 953/116691, August 2012